1095

HOW TO BRIEF A CASE

An Introduction to Legal Reasoning

BY PROFESSOR JOHN DELANEY

DRAWINGS BY ANNE BURGESS

Library of Congress Catalog Card No. 83-072289

First Printing August, 1983
Second Printing September, 1984
Third Printing August, 1986

Published by
Delaney Publications
P.O. Box 404
Bogota, New Jersey 07603-0404
(201-836 2543)

About the Author

Professor John Delaney has taught at the New York University School of Law since 1969 and more recently has taught at the new City University of New York Law School at Queens College. *How To Brief A Case, An Introduction To Legal Reasoning,* has emerged from these years of teaching and of observing common mistakes committed by beginning and other law students. Professor Delaney has been the general editor of ten legal books and has authored two other books, *Criminal Law, A Problem Solving Approach* (1986), and *How To Do Your Best on Law School Exams* (1982). Prior to teaching, Professor Delaney conducted approximately one thousand trials and has written and argued more than one hundred and fifty appeals.

For My Beloved Parents

Valentine - Who fought for the freedom of Ireland.

Elizabeth - Who fought for the freedom of her sons.

ACKNOWLEDGMENTS

I wish first to acknowledge the assistance of Professor Lisa H. Blitman of the New York Law School. Professor Blitman's valuable ideas, unremitting encouragement and critical evaluations have extended throughout the entire span of the project. Anne Burgess' brillant and witty drawings adorn this book and the New Yorker magazine.

Professor Susan Tucker, Director of the First Year Writing Program at the New York University Law School, contributed ideas and a substantive editing which has materially strengthened the book. Professor Liaquat Naz of the Washburn University Law School in Topeka, Kansas reviewed initial drafts of the book and deepened my understanding. Professor Robert Pugsley of the Southwestern University Law School in Los Angeles, California aided in the substantive review of the book. Professor John Sexton of the New York University Law School clarified issues. Harold Marcus of New York University, a novelist and a poet, suggested the idea of the book and provided insight.

Johanna DeNiet typed the manuscript with her usual impressive competence and encouraged me with her support and grace. Kathy Morahan's valuable copy editing deserves special mention. Lora Eiholzer and Marie Lapidus produced the manuscript with word processing magic and cheerfulness.

I acknowledge too the assistance of Larry Abramson, Bill Bernstein, Charles E. Blitman, Diane McClain Blitman, Nan Blitman, Nathan H. Blitman, Victor Essien, Jesse Kasowitz, Frank Llewellyn and Christina Thomas. I also acknowledge that my able students at the New York University Law School have taught me much about legal reasoning over the last fifteen years. Any mistakes or weaknesses, however, are solely my responsibility.

Finally, I must mention the affectionate encouragement of my daughters, Jacqueline and Joanie.

July, 1983

TABLE OF CONTENTS

INTRODUCTION

This book shows you how to brief a case. To show you briefing, it is necessary to introduce you to legal reasoning. Why? Remember what Blake said:

> The cosmos is in a grain of sand.

The cosmos of legal reasoning is in the technique of briefing. It is impossible therefore to learn how to brief without learning something about legal reasoning -- about learning to read, think, talk and write like a lawyer. Hence, the first chapter in this book is less about the technique of briefing and more about why briefing is important:

- -- to enable you to understand cases
- -- to help you understand what happens in class and why
- -- to introduce you to the basic skills necessary for legal reasoning
- -- to get you on the right track and to avoid unnecessary confusion

In Chapter I, I therefore present forty answers to commonly asked questions about law and the first year of law school.

In Chapter II, I present a six-step approach to briefing cases. Detailed guidelines are explained for accomplishing each step. Application of the six-step approach with the guidelines is demonstrated with a short, relatively simple, appellate case, McBoyle v. United States. Applying the six-step approach with the guidelines, an excellent brief of McBoyle is detailed. A contrasting, poor brief of McBoyle is then set forth. My comments detail the reasons why the first brief is excellent and why the second brief is poor. Basic functions of a court which are exemplified in McBoyle are explained. To aid you in beginning to learn which issues may be reviewed on appeal and which may not be, I succinctly detail a series of issues which were not considered and decided in McBoyle and briefly explain why they were not. In a final segment, I define a number of legal terms applied by the court in McBoyle.

The basic pattern of Chapter II is then repeated in chapters III through V. In each chapter, I present a different appellate case (or two) and ask you to apply the six-step approach to briefing with guidelines. Excellent and some poor briefs are set forth. Basic functions of a court illustrated in each case are explained as well as issues not raised and considered. Each chapter concludes with additional definitions of legal terms applied in the case(s) briefed. As you brief these cases, you are also being introduced to legal reasoning, the first priority of the first year of law school.

Too many first-year students misconceive the nature and purpose of law and law school. Most beliefs of beginning students about law school are false or at least misleading. These misconceptions lead to an enormous waste of studying time, blunders in class, exacerbation of beginner's confusion, and a defective preparation for exams. Remember: well started is half done. This short book is designed to get you well started.

How To Use This Book

The ideal way to benefit from this book is as follows:

First, before starting law school, or as soon as possible, read the book through for an overview. Skip over, however, the examples of excellent and poor briefs in chapters II through V.

Second, read Chapter I several times as carefully as you can. Then study the McBoyle case set forth in Chapter II and the suggested guideline process for briefing. Brief McBoyle. Scrutinize the excellent and poor briefs presented and my comments explaining why these briefs are excellent and poor. Compare your brief of McBoyle with the excellent and poor briefs set forth in Chapter II. Don't worry about the quality of your initial effort. Study also the sections on Functions of the Court Exemplified in McBoyle, Issues Not Considered and Decided in McBoyle, and Additional Definitions. Study also the illustration and explanation at the end of Chapter II of the various items typically set forth at the beginning of a case (e.g., caption, citation, headnote, etc.).

Third, apply the case briefing process detailed in Chapter II to the Port Huron case in Chapter III. Compare your brief of Port Huron with the excellent and poor briefs detailed in Chapter III. Don't be discouraged; all beginner's briefs are forgettable. The process of writing awkward, mistake-filled briefs is the path from darkness to light. Study the sections on Functions of the Court Exemplified in Port Huron, Issues Not Considered and Decided in Port Huron, and Additional Definitions.

Fourth, repeat the process with chapters IV and V.

Fifth, at this point examine again all your briefs and contrast them with the excellent and poor briefs. Which features of the excellent briefs are reflected in your briefs? Which features of the poor briefs are reflected in your briefs. Correcting and perfecting presupposes diagnosis. Diagnosis requires careful contrasting.

Sixth, in the first weeks and months of law school, your professors will stress many of the points emphasized in this book. Use the explanations in this book (e.g., what is a principle of law [pp. 8-9], what is a policy [pp. 9-10], what is the principle of a case [p. 75]) to clarify what is unclear. Finally, read the entire book through again after a month or six weeks of classes. Since you'll know much more at that time, you'll see much more in the chapters.

For Teachers

In teaching first-year students at the New York University Law School, I have emphasized that one of my objectives was to bring students from their beginners' level of confusion about cases and legal reasoning to my advanced, sophisticated level of confusion. I intended the remark as only somewhat facetious. I meant to convey the thought that sophistication in the art and craft of legal reasoning is a life-long task. Twenty-three years of lawyering activity, including a thousand trials, one hundred fifty appeals, extensive law-reform activities, and full-time teaching for ten years, has convinced me of the truth of this thought -- and of the following principles which underly this book.

1. Law is a process of reasoning for decision-making about particular controversies. True, it's more than this, but this definition orients beginning students to the overriding priority of first year.

2. The first priority of the first year of law school is the learning of the skills necessary for legal reasoning.

3. It is not knowledge in itself that is imperative but, rather, knowledge filtered through these skills that is imperative for law school and for lawyering.

4. It is important to begin systematically with the basics of legal reasoning.

5. It is important to proceed beyond the basics -- to introduce an intellectual framework that explains what judges actually do in case reasoning.

6. This framework requires introducing students early to the flexibility and resourcefulness of lawyerly argument and of judicial decision-making, including modes of reasoning based on the principle of a case and broad and narrow constructions of a case holding and precedent.

7. Legal reasoning in cases is a gestalt; the parts are only intelligible in light of each other and of the whole. Hence, a holistic perspective is a sine qua non for comprehending key facts, the procedural history, the issue(s), the holding(s), the judgment, the types of legal reasoning applied, and what each case adds to prior cases already deciphered.

These principles do not emerge from interpretation of my dreams. They emerge from my experience including my debt of gratitude to these giants of twentieth-century jurisprudence who are my intellectual mentors for the purpose of this book: Karl Llewellyn, Jerome Frank, Edward Levi, Benjamin Cardozo, and Felix Frankfurter.

Finally, it may be helpful to understand what I attempt in this book by appreciating what I do not attempt. The book is not about legal research. Nor is it about legal writing in any systematic way. Nor is it about statutory construction in any exhaustive manner. It is about briefing a case and about an introduction to legal reasoning.

Any comments and suggestions concerning this book will be appreciated.

INTRODUCTION

The questions and answers in this chapter are about the fundamentals, not the complexities and exceptions. As a beginner, it is vital that you learn basics before you tackle complexities and exceptions. Otherwise, massive confusion is your destiny. Hence, in these initial questions, I have assumed that you have almost no knowledge of our legal system. I have striven to write concise answers and to resist the temptation to elaborate.

Law: What It Is and Is Not

I. What is law?

You may be surprised to know that there is no single definition of law which commands complete agreement. I suggest that, as a beginner, you embrace the following definition:

> Law is a process of legal reasoning for decision-making about particular controversies.

Why embrace this definition? Because it is defensible both in principle and in practice. More importantly, it sheds light on what the first year of law school is about. In the first year, the overriding emphasis is on teaching you to read, think, talk and write like a lawyer. To do this, you must develop a set of skills which will enable you to do legal reasoning for decision-making about particular controversies. The suggested definition of law matches the overriding emphasis of the first year.

II. What the first year of law school is not.

To understand what you do in the first year of law school, it may help to know what you will not do.

1. You will not participate in lengthy class explorations of:

-- justice and the requirements of a just society

-- abstract philosophical and ethical questions

-- economic and sociological theories

-- social science research methods, reports and data

-- political issues

Indeed, many of your professors will react negatively to student responses which reflect these "frequencies" of knowledge and analysis because they want to orient you to a legal frequency of knowledge and analysis. They seek to have you read, think, talk and write like a lawyer, not like a philosopher, ethicist, economist, sociologist, researcher or politician.

III. What are the authoritative sources and types of law?

For your purposes in the first year, the main sources and types of law are:

A) Statutes

B) Cases

C) State and federal constitutions

D) Regulations

IV. What is a statute?

A statute is a particular law, or a body of laws, enacted by a state or federal legislature in conformity with the procedures required by its constitution, state or federal. Such procedures include the usual requirements of majority vote and approval by the governor or President. Examples of statutes include:

-- state penal codes

-- the federal penal code

-- state commercial codes

-- increases or decreases in state or federal taxes

-- a state's adoption of "no-fault" divorce and car insurance

-- the Federal War Powers Act

-- appropriations of state or federal funds

-- abolition of mandatory retirement for federal or state workers

V. What is a case?

In a general sense, a case is any judicial or administrative proceeding in which facts of a controversy are presented in technical legal form for decision-making. The object of such a proceeding is to enforce rights and remedy wrongs. A plaintiff is the party (individual or group) who initiates a case. A defendant is the party (individual or group) who responds. Examples are cases:

-- seeking money damage for breach of contract

-- seeking money damages for injuries in a car accident (tort negligence)

-- prosecuting a defendant for robbery (or any other crime)

-- seeking a divorce, legal separation, child custody, or child support

-- seeking an order from a court directing certain action or forbearance from action by an individual or by any public or private group (an injunction)

In one more specific sense, a case is also the opinion and decision of an appellate court deciding appeals in any of the above-mentioned matters.

A case has two specific functions:

1. it authoritatively decides the particular controversy -- e.g., A gets money damages from B for B's breach of contract

2. it establishes a precedent, or a possible precedent, for the resolution of future controversies with similar facts and issues.

The parties to a case (A and B) are interested in the first function, which determines their rights and duties. As a law student, however, your interest is primarily in the second, precedent-setting function. Much of what you do in class concerns this second function.

VI. What is a constitution?

It is a fundamental political and legal charter for the people of a particular state which is approved by the people (e.g., the Constitution of California) or for the nation (the Federal Constitution). Sometimes called the fundamental law, a constitution defines the character of government by specifying the nature and extent of sovereign power; by distributing this sovereign power (separation of powers); and by prescribing basic principles for the exercise of this power by the three branches of government: the executive, the legislative, and the judiciary. A constitution also typically enumerates the basic rights of the people (a Bill of Rights).

VII. <u>What is a regulation?</u>

Like a case or statute or constitutional provision, a regulation also has the status of law. A regulation is a legal rule authorized by statute (e.g., the Securities Act) and issued by an executive agency (e.g., the Securities and Exchange Commission) for the governance of matters within the authority of the agency (e.g., stocks, bonds, stock exchanges, selling condominiums in interstate commerce). Regulations are used to enforce the statute and are usually more specific than the statute.

<u>Briefing and the Case Method</u>

VIII. <u>What is a brief of a case?</u>

Very simply, it is an organized, written summary of the important elements of a written opinion. Briefing cases is comparable to diagramming sentences: the parts of a case brief (facts, procedural history, issue, holding, judgment, and reasoning) are analogous to the parts of a sentence (subject, verb, object, modifiers). Briefing, or summarizing, the parts of a case is a way to understand the whole.

Distinguish this meaning of a brief from a second meaning which refers to the formal, written argument submitted to a court at motion, during trial, or on appeal.

IX. <u>What is the case method?</u>

It is a method designed to teach legal reasoning for decision-making (including the substantive law) by analyzing many <u>appellate opinions</u> from state and federal appellate courts. It is the dominant pedagogic model used by law schools, particularly in the first year. Be aware that trial courts generally do not write opinions.

<u>The Common Law System</u>

X. <u>What is the common law system?</u>

It is a distinctive system of law, originated in England hundreds of years ago, in which the king's <u>judges made the law</u> throughout the king's realm by deciding numerous cases which came before them. Earlier cases became <u>precedents</u> for deciding later cases with similar facts and issues. These cases accumulated over centuries into a vast body of case law. For a long time, the common law was primarily such judge-made case law. In the last century and especially in recent decades, statutory law has mushroomed and is at least as important as case law. The common law system today incorporates a focus on both cases and statutes. In fact, a great number of cases apply and interpret statutes.

The common law is the system of law in England, in the United States, and in the other, former English colonies. In the majority of countries, however, the civil law and socialist legal systems prevail. In the civil law system, judges' decisions in cases do not become precedents and cases do not accumulate into case law. The socialist legal system reflects the civil law system and also expresses Marxist conceptions of the state, society, and the economy. In all three legal systems, important variations exist from country to country (the United States and England; France and Germany; the Soviet Union and Poland).

Court System

XI. What is a trial court?

A trial court, state or federal, consists of a judge with or without a jury and performs four basic functions in the administration of legal justice within our governmental system of separation of powers (judiciary, executive and legislature):

1. It determines the facts that are in conflict (fact-finding) in particular controversies that are brought before it in technical legal form. It decides which witnesses are credible (believable) and which are not, who said what to whom and who did what to whom, and when. This fact-finding occurs in cases which span the spectrum from criminl law to commercial law, to torts, to copyright, etc.

2. It determines which rules of law from which areas of law are applicable to the particular facts presented (law-finding).

3. It applies the rules to the facts (law-application) to decide the specific dispute presented to the court. The result is a judgment of the court (a decision of the controversy).

4. It does all of the above applying a prescribed procedure which guides pre-trial, trial and post-trial proceedings (civil procedure or criminal procedure).

Trial courts are either courts of general jurisdiction, which have power to consider and decide any authorized civil or criminal case brought before it by private lawyers and public prosecutors, or courts of limited jurisdiction, which have power to consider and decide only limited types of cases (e.g., Traffic Court; Family Court; Criminal Court; Probate Court [wills and estates]). In many states, the court of general jurisdiction is called the Superior Court. In New York, however, it is called the Supreme Court. In other states, it is called the Circuit Court or the District Court.

In our court system, trial courts are either part of the state court system which exists in each state, or part of the national, federal court system. The federal court of general jurisdiction is called the United States District Court. Each state has one or more federal district courts.

XII. What is an appellate court?

An appellate court, state or federal, hears appeals from the trial courts within its jurisdiction (its purview) in the administration of legal justice. Except in unusual cases, appellate courts accept the facts as determined (found) by the trial court. Appellate courts assess and decide claims that the trial court committed legal error. This is called an appeal. In deciding appeals, appellate courts do not ordinarily consider such factual questions as the credibility of witnesses, what happened on a particular day at a particular place. All of that is resolved by the trial court.

Examples of claims of legal error raised on appeal and decided by appellate courts include: prejudicial rulings by the trial court in admitting or excluding testimony and other evidence; mistakes in selecting and applying rules; insufficient evidence to prove the case (e.g., negligent tort; intentional tort; breach of contract; arson); violation of state or federal constitutional provisions.

In many states, the highest court within the state is called the Supreme Court. In New York, however, it is called the Court of Appeals, and in Massachusetts it is called the Supreme Judicial Court. In addition, many states have intermediate appellate courts.

Like the trial courts, the appellate courts are either part of the state court system in each state or part of the national, federal court system. In the federal court system, the highest court is the United States Supreme Court. In addition, there is an intermediate appellate court, the United States Court of Appeals, which is organized on a regional basis into eleven circuits.

Two Basic Common Law Doctrines

XIII. What is res judicata?

The doctrine of res judicata (a "thing which has been adjudicated") means that once a particular claim is finally decided by a court (including appeals) with jurisdiction over the claim and the parties, the court's judgment, and the factual and legal issues underlying it, are considered conclusively decided and may not be relitigated by the parties.

The doctrine of res judicata serves the policy interest of barring endless relitigation of claims and the policy interest of judicial economy. Res judicata is a doctrine which is strictly applied by the courts.

XIV. What is stare decisis?

Very simply, the common law doctrine of stare decisis ("stand by the decision") means that the decision of a court in one case provides a precedent (i.e., a standard) for the decision of future cases with like or similar facts and issues in the same or inferior courts within a particular jurisdiction. The rule or principle of law necessary to decide the facts and issues presented in one case provides a precedent for deciding future cases with similar facts and issues. The doctrine of stare decisis serves a number of fundamental policy interests in the common law system, including:

A) one meaning of justice: like treatment of like cases

B) a consistent, continuous, and coherent body of case law

C) a reasonable degree of predictability so that lawyers can counsel clients and so that we can all legally arrange our commercial and personal affairs with reasonable confidence about the future

D) authority for judges to build upon past experience, thereby eliminating the need to reconsider old rules of law in each new case

E) fettering the choices and discretion of judges and juries within a framework of the rule of law rather than the rule of whim, arbitrariness, bias or paternalism

While stare decisis is a wellspring of our law (in Cardozo's words, "the everyday working rule of our law"), it is not absolute. Exceptions exist and will be illustrated in Chapter V (pp. 111-130).

Binding Precedent

A binding precedent means that a decision of a court in a prior case controls the decision in future cases with like or similar facts and issues for both the deciding court and for all inferior courts within the same jurisdiction. Thus, a decision of the Supreme Court of California is a binding precedent for future cases with like or similar facts and issues which are decided by the Supreme Court of California and by all inferior courts in California. A binding precedent is both a norm and a prediction. It is a norm because the decision of future cases with similar facts and issues in the same or inferior courts within a particular jurisdiction should be controlled by the precedent. It is also a prediction that such future cases will be controlled by the precedent.

Persuasive Precedent

A persuasive precedent means that a decision of a court in a prior case may be accepted or rejected by a court in a new case, even though the facts and issues in the new case are similar. For example, a New

York court has discretion to accept or reject the precedent set by the Supreme Court of California in a case with similar facts and issues. For the New York court, the California precedent is merely persuasive, not binding. The reason why the California precedent is not controlling in New York is that California and New York are separate jurisdictions. California courts do not have the power to decide New York law, and New York courts do not have the power to decide California law.

Substantive Law

XV. What is a rule of law?

A) an authoritive legal standard

B) of general application

C) requiring action or forbearance

D) used by courts and administrative tribunals

E) as a norm

F) in deciding the legal significance

G) of the particular facts

H) presented in individual cases

The most important sources of rules for the first year of law school are: 1) the laws passed by the state and federal legislatures; and 2) the body of common law (judge-made law) embodied in many thousands of cases in each state. An example of a statutory rule, imposed by a legislature, is the requirement that drivers of cars and trucks obtain driving licenses. An example of a case law rule, imposed by judge-made law, is the requirement that such drivers exercise the degree of care in driving that an ordinary, prudent or reasonable person would use (tort law). An example of statutory and case law rules operating together is the requirement that such drivers refrain from driving in a criminally negligent manner.

In addition, in a few first-year courses, such as constitutional law, criminal law and civil procedure, you study principles set forth in the Federal Constitution. Typically, you'll study regulatory law (administrative law, securities or federal taxation) in the second and third years.

XVI. What is a principle of law?

A principle has the characteristics of a rule (see prior definition); and, in addition, a principle:

1. has a more fundamental status in law than a rule

2. has a broader or more inclusive scope or reach than a rule

3. may be used as a basis for creating rules

4. is sometimes used by a judge to select which one of the two or more arguably applicable rules should be applied in a particular case

In our system of law, some fundamental principles are explicitly specified in the Constitution of the United States, including:

-- the principle of due process

-- the principle of equal protection of the law

-- the principles of freedom of speech, press and assembly

Other federal constitutional principles are derived from those which are explicitly specified and then embodied in the case law of the U.S. Supreme Court, including:

-- the principle that each person has a right of privacy, derived from the first, fourth and other amendments

-- the principle that vague criminal statutes are a violation of due process

Many other important principles are not derived from state or federal constitutions but from state and federal statutes and case law, including:

-- the principle that private contracts between individuals must not violate public policy (case law)

-- the principle that core crimes (e.g., murder, robbery, rape, arson) must have a criminal intent requirement (case law and statute)

It is important to realize that just as rules exist at varying levels of concreteness, principles (and policies) exist at varying levels of breadth. Law spans the spectrum from extreme concreteness (e.g., the rule that an answer to a complaint must be filed within twenty days) to extreme breadth (e.g., the principle of due process).

XVII. What is a legal policy?

A policy (also known as a policy purpose or policy objective) is the interest or end expressed or served by a rule or principle.

For example, the prohibition of murder by rules and principles based on statutes and case law which express and serve the policy interest (or purpose) of protecting the life of each member of the society. The prohibition of rape by rules, also based on statutes and case law, expresses and serves the policy interest (or objective) of protecting bodily integrity. The various rules and principles governing the making of a contract (e.g., offer, acceptance and consideration) express and serve the policy purposes (or interests) of freedom of contract and promotion of commerce. The tort rules spelling out the requirements for establishing negligence express and serve the policy objective (or purposes or interests) of fairness and monetary compensation for injuries due to the carelessness of others. And lastly, the rules of civil procedure, again based on statutes and case law, express and promote the policy purpose, among others, of equal access to the courts.

In addition, a broad policy purpose is sometimes applied directly (like a rule or principle) as a norm to decide individual cases -- e.g., the policy norm in a child custody case of promoting the best interests of the child.

XVIII. Is there consistency in the use of rule, principle and policy?

No. As I stated in my book, How To Do Your Best On Law School Exams:

> Do not expect scientific precision and consistency here. What some cases and professors describe as a rule may be called a principle (or doctrine) or policy by others. Principle and policy are sometimes used interchangeably. If you do not expect consistency in these labels, you will not be disappointed and confused. Knowing these labels is far less important than understanding the rules, principles and policies and being able to apply them correctly. A safe approach for you is to follow your professor's usage in each course.

Moreover, many cases are poorly crafted; the quality of the legal writing is obscure, confused and confusing, making it difficult to spot the issue, identify the holding, and make sense of the reasoning. If you find a case confusing, one strong possibility is that you, as a beginner, are confused -- and you must struggle to understand. Another possibility, however, is that the confusion is intrinsic to the case. Learning the difference is a skill to be acquired by analyzing and discussing hundreds of cases. Incidentally, the fact that a case is unclear provides no escape: you must, nevertheless, extricate the relevant facts, specify the procedural history, identify the issue and the holding, and make as much sense of the reasoning as possible.

Skills for Legal Reasoning

XIX. What are the basic skills required for legal reasoning?

-- extricating the key facts

-- spotting issues

-- selecting rules and principles

-- applying rules, especially by interweaving of key facts with the elements of rules

-- adroitly using policy

-- writing in a lawyerly fashion

Legal reasoning is circular. The necessary skills are like a web; they interconnect and overlap. Hence, while skills can be individually identifed and analyzed, they must be practiced and learned as a configuration.

XX. What is extricating key facts?

Extricating key facts is a process of selecting from all the mass of facts presented in a written opinion, by a client, or on an exam, those particular facts which have the most legal significance. Facts or a combination of facts which have the most legal significance are those which establish the elements of a legal rule and therefore require or permit application of that rule. Key facts are those facts which raise an issue of law. For example, the fact that A and B, business partners, are arguing about how profits should be split presents a business question which has no legal significance; such a fact is therefore not legally relevant, though it may be relevant from a business perspective to an MBA student or relevant psychologically (revealing unconscious childhood conflicts) to A's and B's psychotherapists. But, the fact that A then declares, "I've had enough," and shoots and kills B is a fact having legal significance because the rules and principles of criminal law, which proscribe murder, and of tort law, which proscribe assault and battery, attach to the fact that A shot and killed B and make that fact legally relevant, a key fact.

XXI. What is issue-spotting?

Issue-spotting is the corollary of extricating key facts. A legal issue is simply a question(s) raised by the key facts about their legal significance. To use the above illustration, while no legal issue is raised by A's and B's merely arguing, as a beginning law student questions should spring into your mind about the existence of a legal issue when you read that A said, "I've had enough" and shot and killed B. In criminal law the issue could be identified as follows: Did A's saying "I've had enough," and shooting and killing B make A liable for intentional murder? Or, in torts, the issue could be specified as follows: Did A's saying "I've had enough", and shooting and killing B, make A liable for the intentional torts of assault and battery?

As these simple examples illustrate, the formulation of an issue in a one-sentence question incorporates the key facts (or some of them) and points to an applicable rule of law. Issue-spotting connects the key facts with the rule to be applied.

XXII. What is selection of a rule?

Judges in deciding cases, lawyers in arguing cases, law students in studying for class and exams select applicable rules to apply to the relevant facts. To illustrate, when A and B argue over the split of profits, it is not necessary to select any rule to resolve an issue posed by such facts. Why? There are no legally relevants facts which raise an issue requiring selection of a rule of law. A and B's business argument does not pose a legal conflict. When A, however, proceeds to shoot and kill B, these are relevant facts which raise a legal issue in criminal law (is A in shooting and killing B liable for intentional murder?) and which lead to selection of the applicable rule. The rule to be selected in light of these facts is intentional murder, which has five elements:

A) intent to kill

B) manifested in an

C) act which

D) causes, factually and legally

E) the death of another person

Notice that this rule, as almost all rules, is composed of elements. To know a rule is to know its elements and to be able to specify them precisely, without surplusage and without omissions.

XXIII. What is rule-application, especially interweaving of facts with elements of rules?

Interweaving is the blending together of the key facts with the elements of an applicable rule. By so doing, a student and a lawyer demonstrate that the rule selected is applicable because there are sufficient facts to prove each element of the rule. For example, if A insults B, you know from studying tort cases and a tort hornbook that the applicable rule is "mere words of insult, even violent insults, are not in themselves actionable." Interweaving the key facts with the rule is illustrated below:

A is not liable to B in intentional tort.

> The rule is that mere words of insult, even violent insults, are not in themselves actionable. When A insults B, these are mere words of insult and give rise to no legal liability. While the facts do not spell out "violent insults," the reasoning and result would be identical.

When A, however, says to B, "I've had enough" and shoots and kills B, you interweave these facts with the five elements of the rule of intentional murder, as follows:

"A" is liable for intentional murder. When A says to B -- "I've had enough" and shoots B -- A's intent to kill B is plain. The act of shooting also manifests A's intent to kill and fulfills the requirement of an act. When B then dies from the shooting, the remaining requirements of factual and legal causation and the death of another person are easily met.

Interweaving is the chief skill of rule application.

XXIV. What is adroit use of policy?

Adroit use of policy in an opinion, on an exam, or in practice stems from an understanding of the nature and function of policy (see pp. 9-10). If you see policies as the ends or interests served by applying rules and principles, you will have a sharper and deeper understanding of legal reasoning and will be better able to decide whether or not a specific rule applies. You will be able to buttress your rule application, especially in close cases, with a succinct reference to the policy served by a particular rule. In novel fact situations, you will be able to apply the policy directly or to argue for application of a new rule to be applied in light of the policy to be served.

Contrary to what some first-year students think, policy is not your latest political hallucination -- or mine. Legal policies should not be equated with political policies. Most legal policy is entrenched in the law, embodied in cases and statutes. Many first-year professors stress such policy, not just rules and principles. The best way to learn to identify and use legal policies adroitly is to pinpoint how judges use policies in opinions and to pay close attention to your professors' comments on such usage.

XXV. What is lawyerly writing?

Lawyerly writing, the final skill required for legal reasoning, is necessary to apply the first five skills. These five skills -- extricating the key facts; issue-spotting; selecting rules; applying rules; and using policy -- are neither abstract nor independent of each other. You demonstrate that you possess these skills by displaying them in lawyerly talk in class and lawyerly writing on exams and in legal memoranda.

Lawyerly writing is:

-- organized

-- purposeful

-- direct

-- clear

-- concise

-- complete

-- logical (avoiding contradictions, inconsistencies and non-sequiturs)

-- persuasive

Lawyerly writing is not:

-- rambling

-- verbose

-- fancy, pretentious or pompous

-- conclusory or sweeping

-- cryptic or cursory

-- abstract or academic

-- only factual

-- only about rules, principles and policies

-- the same as historical, sociological, philosophical, ethical, economic, literary or scientific analysis.

The First Year

XXVI. Why is the first year of law school formidable?

It's like being immersed suddenly in a foreign country and struggling with a strange language. You have to learn a new vocabulary (legal terms), a new grammar (skills in legal reasoning), and conversation (application for decision-making). Some confusion and awkwardness are inevitable.

More concretely:

1. Many of the words in cases are purely legal and you must learn their meanings one by one (e.g., res ipsa locquitur, sua sponte, demurrer, mandamus, certiorari, mens rea, actus reus).

2. Many of the words used in cases which have an ordinary meaning in English also have a technical, legal meaning which is the meaning intended in the cases (e.g., motion, answer, malice, provocation, the reasonable man, intent, trespass, equitable).

3. When you begin, you can spot words in the first category, but you won't know immediately which ordinary English words have a special legal meaning (second category).

4. Many of the words in the first two categories have multiple legal meanings. While a legal dictionary is helpful, you may have difficulty in the beginning selecting which of the multiple meanings defined in the dictionary is the particular meaning intended in a specific case. Gradually, as you learn these meanings one by one, the mist will transform into clear categories.

5. Since law is legal reasoning for decision-making, it isn't enough to understand the above-mentioned, basic skills abstractly. A skill is a habit of performance, not simply an abstract understanding. These skills can only be developed by practice over a substantial period of time.

XXVII. In developing these basic skills of legal reasoning, am I learning to read, think, talk and write like a lawyer?

Exactly -- and this is the first priority in the first year of law school. Indeed, it is fruitful for you to visualize yourself as learning legal reasoning by studying torts, contracts, criminal law, civil procedure, etc. If, over a period of time, you develop and internalize these basic skills -- make them part of yourself -- you'll use some of these skills each day you work as a lawyer. You'll gradually perfect a lawyerly approach to any legal issue -- your reading, thinking, talking and writing will become more precise and vigorous. This is one of the principal objectives of law school. In contrast, contrary to what you believe, much of the subject matter you learn in specific courses (e.g., criminal law, torts) will eventually fade, with the obvious exception of areas of your practice (e.g., wills and estates, real estate, or commercial law).

Role of Knowledge

XXVIII. You don't emphasize knowledge -- I though law school meant learning the law?

Not in the sense of defining law as essentially a series of rules, principles and policies to be memorized and regurgitated upon proper cue. Not in the sense of seeing a law student and a lawyer as human computers to be programmed (stuffed) with thousands of statutes and cases in thirty or more areas of law.

The knowledge that will help you is the knowledge that empowers you to extricate the key facts, spot issues, select rules, interweave, use policy and write in a lawyerly way. It is not knowledge in itself that will help you but knowledge filtered through these basic skills. Knowledge is not an end in itself but a means to the end of legal reasoning for decision-making. Knowledge is, then, absolutely necessary and absolutely insufficient.

The false idea that law and the learning of law are primarily a matter of memorizing and regurgitating knowledge is a classic, first-year blunder. Avoid it.

Briefing and Skills

XXIX. <u>How does briefing help me to learn and practice the basic legal skills necessary for legal reasoning?</u>

The appellate cases which you brief in law school illustrate the use of the basic skills necessary for legal reasoning. Specifically, in writing an appellate decision, the judge:

-- identifies and marshalls the key facts

-- identifies the legal issue raised by the facts

-- selects the applicable rule of law and incorporates the rule into a holding

-- interweaves the elements of that rule with the key facts

-- sometimes uses policy to buttress the reasoning

-- does all of the above with lawyerly writing

Each case is a vivid demonstration of the basic skills necessary for legal reasoning.

In briefing appellate cases, you identify and analyze each part of the decision which exemplifies the above-listed, basic skills. For example, you identify key facts, spot issues, identify holdings, etc., as they are presented in the case. Therefore, in briefing these cases and working with their component parts (e.g., facts, issues, holdings), you practice the basic skills necessary for legal reasoning. The cases present a veritable Milky Way of legal reasoning for decision-making. Case briefing is your telescope.

XXX. <u>Am I supposed to learn all about legal reasoning from briefing cases?</u>

No. Briefing cases is one core means for deciphering cases. Other methods include the Socractic method in class, class discussion, lectures, writing exercises, moot court, and study groups.

XXXI. <u>Do these basic skills of legal reasoning apply in doing other legal tasks?</u>

Yes. They apply in:

-- class discussion

-- law school and bar exams

-- written and oral argument for motions, trials, and appeals

-- everyday legal practice including assessing the merit of cases, writing legal memoranda, marshalling facts, etc.

XXXII. <u>How does briefing cases help me prepare for class?</u>

Although many beginning students don't realize it, the dominant priority in first-year classes is the teaching of legal reasoning by stressing the basic skills. Typically, students are asked questions about the core elements of the case (facts, procedure, issue, holding, judgment and reasoning). Your case brief provides the foundation for your responses. Moreover, if you are not called upon and do not volunteer, your brief also enables you to follow the questions, answers, discussion and lecture.

In addition, teachers ask hypotheticals -- questions about the issues raised in a case or in a series of cases. What you have learned from case briefing enables you to respond and to understand the responses of others and your professors' comments.

Moreover, your professors will stress reconciling and synthesizing of a number of cases. What you have learned from briefing these cases enables you to participate in this process.

XXXIII. <u>What is reconciling and synthesizing of cases?</u>

To learn lawyerly reading, thinking, talking and writing by means of the case law method requires concentrating on a chain of related cases, not simply on individual cases, one by one. Each case is a link in a chain of reasoning. It is this linkage that makes each case important in the case law process and that underlies your professor's insistent question -- what does this case add (meaning why is this case significant in light of the rest of the relevant cases). Once you understand the chain of reasoning in a group of cases, you are able to understand each case more deeply and more sharply. John Donne's line -- "no man is an island" -- is paralleled: no case is an island.

The technique for identifying and analyzing the chain of reasoning in a group of related cases is called reconciling and synthesizing cases. It is a legal application of the logic of analysis by comparison, which stresses similarities and differences. The doctrine of <u>stare decisis</u> (see pp. 7-8) makes the determination of similarities or differences the crucial step in legal reasoning. Your professor's questions will pinpoint similarities and differences in the facts, the issue posed, rule selection, the holding, and the analysis. Through this relentless questioning and answering, you unravel the meaning of a group of cases and you hone your basic skills, including your knowledge of substantive law. You therefore increase your legal reasoning ability and your confidence.

XXXIV. What is the Socratic method?

Inspired by Socrates, the great Greek philosopher, the Socratic method is a series of professorial questions and student answers designed to unravel a particular case and a series of cases. The questioning is designed to teach students the substantive law by practicing the basic skills. Many of the questions focus explicitly on these skills: e.g., what are the facts; what is the issue; what is the holding; what is the court's reasoning? Other questions typically focus on contrasts and similarities with prior cases: e.g., can you reconcile this holding and reasoning with the holding and reasoning in the prior case? In addition to the Socratic method, you will encounter substantial lecturing and discussion and, if you are lucky, a bit of wit.

XXXV. In addition to briefing cases, what else should I do to prepare for class?

Read the sections in the hornbook recommended by your professor which cover the issues presented in the assigned class. A good hornbook offers an organized, systematic presentation of the issues and relevant rules, principles and policies. It is comparable to a college textbook (e.g., Samuelson on Economics).

If the cases assigned in torts class, for example, cover self-defense issues, read the corresponding section in the recommended hornbook on self-defense. Exercise self-discipline: read only this section. Otherwise, you'll risk drowning in materials.

The important advantage in reading such relevant hornbook sections is that you can acquire an overview of the substantive law from basics to complexities. This overview helps you to understand what occurs in class -- the questioning and answering about cases and hypotheticals, and the reconciling and synthesizing of cases.

XXXVI. What is the value of class participation?

The answer is clear if you keep in mind two realities:

A) the first year is primarily designed to teach you legal reasoning -- to read, think, talk and write like a lawyer;

B) the dominant priority in first-year classes is to teach you the basic skills of such reasoning.

By participating in class, you are practicing your listening, thinking and talking like a lawyer. Making mistakes is the norm; in fact, you can't develop the basic skills without making mistakes. Over time, participation aids you to internalize and hone the skills.

XXXVII. What are the disadvantages of learning by the case method?

First, the casebooks do not typically present the issues, rules, principles and policies in a systematic, basics-to-complexities order. In short, the substantive law is often confusingly presented. The disciplined use of a good hornbook, however, is an effective remedy.

Second, the appellate opinions reprinted in casebooks tend to concentrate on the complexities and the numerous exceptions, giving some students a warped, exception-obsessed view of the law. Again, the disciplined study of good hornbooks which present the basics, as well as the complexities and exceptions, is an effective remedy.

Third, a range of fundamental lawyerly skills are not taught, or mostly not taught, with the case method. These include skills in:

A) uncovering facts from clients, witnesses, documents and elsewhere

B) interviewing

C) client counseling

D) negotiating and mediating

E) writing

F) motion, trial and appellate advocacy

G) informal advocacy (e.g., with administrative agencies at federal, state and local levels)

H) working collaboratively with others

I) reflecting on the underlying values implicit in cases and the personal choices inherent in different forms of lawyering

Fortunately, these skills can often be learned in clinical and simulation courses. In clinical courses, you represent, under supervision, actual clients. In simulation courses, you simulate such representation. In addition, you can acquire these skills by part-time paid and volunteer legal work. It is a mistake, however, to undertake such legal work during the first year of full-time law school unless economic pressures allow no alternative.

Statutes

XXXVIII. What is the role of statutes and when do I learn them?

Even with the emphasis on the case method of teaching law in the first year, there is considerable emphasis on statutes. First, one of the principal functions of appellate courts in deciding cases is application and interpretation of statutes. Hence, many cases deal with specific statutes. Second, there is an emphasis on statutes in some first-year courses such as Contracts (the Uniform Commercial Code) and Criminal Law (the Model Penal Code or a particular state penal code). Third, some first-year professors stress statutes much more than others. Lastly, in second and third years, most students take courses with a strong statutory emphasis (e.g., wills and estates; commercial law; New York or Illinois or California Civil Practice).

The Bar Exam

XXXIX. How will briefing help me pass the bar exam?

The best way for you, as a beginner, to prepare for the bar exam is to forget the bar exam. Concentrate on developing your basic skills of legal reasoning which will serve you well in law school, on the bar exam, and in lawyering. To think about the bar exam now is to engage in "crackpot realism." It's like worrying about the twelfth-grade calculus exam as you begin the ninth-grade algebra course.

What Else?

XXXX. In addition to learning how to brief cases as a means of learning the basic skills, what else must I learn as a beginning law student?

1. It isn't enough to learn how to brief cases. You must actually brief them. Intellectual understanding is only a prelude to actually briefing hundreds of cases and thus learning to read, think, talk and write like a lawyer.

2. You must learn the fundamentals of legal research: how to use the law library. Remember that brilliant, experienced lawyers, judges and professors constantly use the law library. In addition, learn, as quickly as you can, how to use computerized legal research systems such as Lexis and Westlaw. They are fun, quick and effective.

3. You must learn to prepare for law exams. They are different from college and graduate school exams and may surprise you. You will not be astonished to learn that I recommend my own 1982 book, How To Do Your Best On Law Exams, which will soon be in a fifth printing and which is available in most law bookstores and in most law libraries. How To Do Your Best On Law School Exams and this book complement each other by embodying common themes, attitudes and methods which I believe will be most helpful to you.

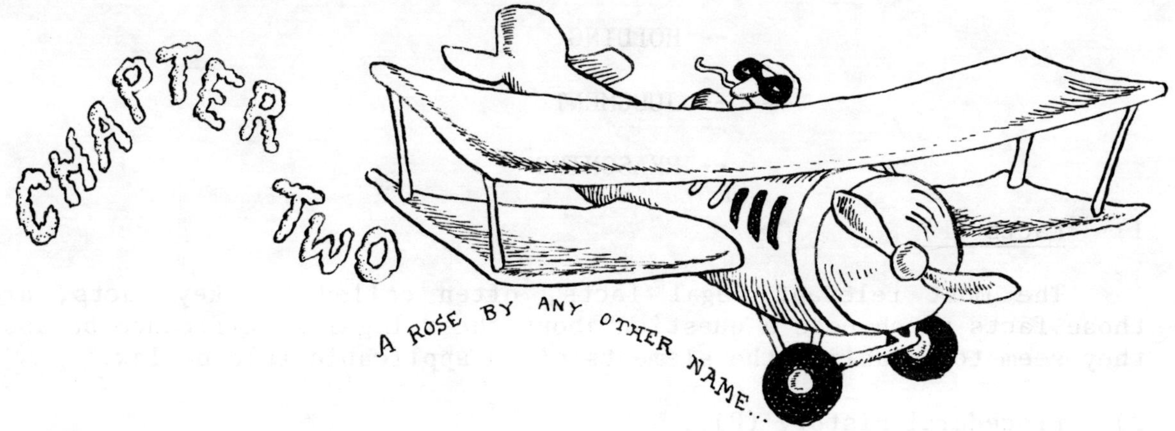

I. INTRODUCTION

What you have learned from studying the questions and answers in the first chapter is at best only a prelude -- a stage setter. It is not enough to know about briefing cases; you must also be able to do it. If at all times you keep in mind that law is legal reasoning for decision-making about particular controversies, you have the right "head set" for developing the necessary legal skills.

In this chapter, I first explain the steps for briefing an appellate case and detail guidelines for performing each step. Next, I demonstrate the briefing process step by step using a short, simple case. An excellent brief and a poor brief are set forth.

I then explain two particular court functions exemplified in this case. I identify the issues not considered and decided by the court's opinion and explain why these issues were not considered. Lastly, the chapter concludes with additional definitions arising mainly from the briefed case and with explanations of the caption, citation and various other typical items which appear at the beginning of a case.

II. STEPS FOR BRIEFING

The first requirement in briefing a case is to read it carefully at least two or three times. As you read, concentrate on the six steps for briefing:

-- FACTS

-- PROCEDURAL HISTORY

-- ISSUE

-- HOLDING

-- JUDGMENT

-- REASONING

1) Facts (F)

The most relevant legal facts, often called the key facts, are those facts which pose a question about their legal significance because they seem to establish the elements of an applicable rule of law.

2) Procedural History (P)

The procedural history of a case identifies which party won at the trial level and which party is appealing now in which appellate court.

3) Issue (I)

The issue(s) in controversy is the question presented by the key facts in light of an apparently applicable rule of law. In order to decide the case, the court must answer the legal question presented by the issue.

4) Holding (H)

A holding is the court's direct response to the issue in controversy. It is that rule of law applied to the key facts of the case which is necessary to decide the particular controversy.

5) Judgment (J)

The judgment is the result or disposition of the case and is usually found at the end of the appellate court's opinion, e.g., "judgment for the plaintiff affirmed" or "judgment for the defendant reversed."

6) Reasoning (R)

The reasoning is the court's explanation and justification for its holding.

Briefing Cases is Like Playing Checkers

Even this initial outline of the six steps for briefing cases demonstrates that the steps overlap and are inextricably interwoven; each step, like each strand in a spider's web, depends on the others. Briefing cases is also like playing checkers or chess. Just as each move in checkers or chess is made in light of both prior moves and future moves and an overall strategy for the game, each step in briefing has meaning both in itself and also as part of a series of steps and an overall approach to the brief.

III. GUIDELINES FOR PERFORMING EACH STEP

I detail below guidelines for performing each of the six steps for briefing. I have broken down each step into its component parts. At first, the application of these guidelines may seem too detailed and complex. If you struggle in the beginning, however, the application of the guidelines will become easy, almost second nature. In struggling, you will also learn about legal reasoning. Learning to apply these guidelines is like learning to drive a car with a manual, "stick" shift. At first, it is perplexing. With practice, however, it becomes almost second nature. In presenting these guidelines, I first list them in capsule form and then elaborate on each one separately. Where the guidelines overlap, I indicate that fact.

Six Guidelines for Extricating the Key Facts

1) Identify parties and their roles.

2) Identify plaintiff's cause-of-action.

3) Identify the element(s) of the cause-of-action which poses the conflict.

4) Identify the facts most relevant to this element(s).

5) Identify defense and its particular element(s) in question.

6) Identify the facts most relevant to this element(s).

1. The parties and their role.

Start by identifying the parties to the case and their roles in the case, both at trial and on appeal. For example, the parties may be the plaintiff-seller against the defendant-buyer in contracts; or the plaintiff-wife against the defendant-husband in tort negligence; or the state (or government) against the defendant in criminal law. Simply use the labels applied by the court to describe the parties. Typically, these are appellant-appellee; petitioner-respondent; plaintiff-defendant; state (or government)-defendant. A word of caution: realize that the defendant at trial may become the appellant (or petitioner or plaintiff) on appeal; the plaintiff (or state) at trial may become the appellee (or respondent or defendant) on appeal. Distinguish the trial and appellate levels and any differences in labels.

2. The plaintiff's cause-of-action.

The cause-of-action is the plaintiff's legal claim against the defendant. Thus, your factual summary should specify the cause-of-action which the plaintiff (or state) alleged at trial against the defendant; e.g., breach of contract, tort negligence, robbery. The court's decision determines the legal rights and duties of the parties arising from that claim.

3.&4. The element(s) at issue and relevant facts.

The factual summary presented in an appellate opinion generally focuses on a particular segment of the facts detailed in the trial court record because many cases on appeal concern a conflict over the existence of a particular element(s) necessary to establish the plaintiff's cause-of-action. The facts relating to this element(s) are often called key facts. The search for the key facts also entails a search for the element(s) of the claim which poses the conflict on appeal. Key facts are those which are crucial for establishing, or not establishing, the element(s) at issue.

For example, in a cause-of-action for damages for breach of contract, the only element in dispute may be the element of acceptance, which is one of the elements necessary to form a contract (offer, acceptance, consideration). The facts about this claimed acceptance, or at least some of them, are key facts. If you can zero in on the element in dispute, you are close to finding the key facts.

5.&6. Any asserted defense, element(s) at issue, and relevant facts.

You repeat the process outlined above in 2), 3) and 4) with regard to any defense emphasized in the appellate court's marshalling of the facts. Again, if you can zero in on the particular element(s) of such defense which is in conflict, you are close to determining the key facts or some of them.

Hints for extricating key facts.

You can often tell from how the appellate court organizes its written opinion and from the language it uses what the court considers to be the key facts. For example, the court may emphasize the key facts by mentioning them first; however, some judges distribute key facts throughout the opinion and others present facts in chronological order so that the facts mentioned first are simply the earliest occurring facts in a series of events and may or may not be the most relevant.

Pay special attention to the court's explicit characterization of which facts it considers most significant; e.g., "it is important...;" or "what is decisive here..." or "the Court determines..." but be careful that what follows specifies facts, not the holding or reasoning. Look too for sheer repetition of certain facts.

Don't be fooled by an appellate court's summary of allegations of fact by the plaintiff or by the defendant at trial; "the plaintiff contended..." or "the defendant maintained...." Such a summary, however, is often followed in the opinion by the court's specification of the key facts upon which it relies.

Procedural History

The purpose of this segment of your brief is to pinpoint the current procedural status of the case. You are already familiar with the first two guidelines.

Five Guidelines for Determining Procedural History

1) Identify parties and their roles.

2) Identify plaintiff's cause of action at trial.

3) Identify trial court's disposition of cause-of-action.

4) Identify which party appealed to which court and the relief requested.

5) Identify any prior action taken by an intermediate appellate court.

1. The parties and their roles at trial and on appeal.

This guideline is the same as the comparable guideline suggested for determining the key facts (see pp. 23-24).

2. The plaintiff's cause-of-action in the trial court.

This guideline is the same as the comparable guideline suggested for determining the key facts (see p. 24), except that you need not focus on the elements of the cause-of-action.

3. The disposition of the plaintiff's cause-of-action in the trial court.

The disposition is the result, that is, who won and who lost what in the trial court. For example, there may have been a judgment for the plaintiff for $40,000 in a tort negligence case, a judgment of conviction of the defendant for robbery in a criminal case, or a judgment dismissing the plaintiff's complaint alleging a cause-of-action for breach of contract.

It's important to identify the exact trial court disposition of the plaintiff's cause-of-action in order to understand the issue in controversy on appeal. Did the trial court, for example, grant the plaintiff or defendant summary judgment in response to a pre-trial motion? Or did the trial court dismiss the plaintiff's cause-of-action during trial because the plaintiff failed to establish a prima facie case? Or did the judge and jury find for the plaintiff or defendant at the conclusion of the trial?

4. Determine who is appealing and for what relief.

The party appealing may be called the plaintiff, the petitioner, or the appellant. The responding party may be called the defendant, the respondent, or the appellee. Identifying which party is asking for exactly what relief helps you to understand the appellate court's response. Usually the party appealing is the losing party in the trial court and usually such party is asking for a reversal of the trial court's judgment. Look at the beginning of the appellate court's opinion for the court's identification of which party is appealing for what relief.

5. Any prior action or disposition by an intermediate appellate court.

Many of the cases you brief will be direct appeals from a trial court. In other cases, however, you brief cases which already have been decided by an intermediate appellate court. Thus, the current case may be an appeal from a judgment of the intermediate appellate court which affirmed or reversed a judgment of the trial court. Know the difference between these two types of appellate cases.

Issue-Spotting

The purpose of this segment of your brief is to spot and specify the issue(s) in controversy in the case on appeal. The issue(s) in controversy is that issue(s) which must be decided by the appellate court to resolve the appeal. Keep in mind that there are many possible issues at pre-trial, trial and appellate stages of a case. Since you are studying appellate court opinions, you will concentrate on the issue(s) in controversy on appeal. Other issues in the case, possibly many, have already been resolved at the trial stage. Issue-spotting is a core lawyerly skill. Issue-spotting in appellate opinions is a necessary step in the cultivation of this core skill.

I suggest the following guidelines for issue-spotting in appellate opinions. You will note that these guidelines are similar to the guidelines for extricating the key facts (see pp. 23-24).

Five Guidelines for Issue-Spotting

1) **Identify plaintiff's cause-of-action and its elements.**

2) **Identify element(s) of cause-of-action which poses the conflict on appeal.**

3) **Identify appellate court's marshalling of the facts.**

4) **Repeat steps 1, 2, and 3 regarding any defense emphasized by Court.**

5) **Formulate the issue(s) in controversy.**

1. The plaintiff's cause-of-action at trial and its elements.

To pinpoint the issue in controversy on appeal, you must first identify the cause-of-action asserted by the plaintiff against the defendant in the trial court (e.g., tort negligence, breach of contract, trespass) and the elements necessary to establish that cause-of-action. These elements are often mentioned in the court's opinion. If not, you can determine them by reading your casebook, a hornbook, a good outline, or from class discussion.

2.&3. The particular element(s) of that cause-of-action which poses the conflict on appeal and the court's marshalling of facts on this element.

Often in appellate opinions the issue in controversy concerns a particular element of the cause-of-action. For example, in the McBoyle case later in this chapter, the issue in controversy arises from one such element. So the court's analysis focuses on that element and the facts pertaining to it. At trial, there may have been a number of issues in conflict which are no longer at issue on appeal. On appeal, therefore, there may be only one main question (one issue in controversy), though in some appellate cases there may be two or three or even more issues.

4. Any defense, its particular element, and marshalling of facts.

The issue(s) in controversy on the appeal may also concern a particular element of a defense asserted by the defendant to the plaintiff's cause-of-action. How do you verify whether or not there is such a defense? The court's opinion provides the answer. Does its marshalling of facts from the trial record focus on a defense (e.g., a claim of contributory negligence to the tort negligence, cause-of-action; a claim that no contract existed to the breach of contract, cause-of-action; or a claim of consent to the trespass cause-of-action)?

5. Formulate the issue in controversy.

The issue in controversy incorporates the key facts in a one sentence question which refers to the cause-of-action (the legal rule) and pinpoints the element(s), or its particular language, which is the source of the conflict between the parties on appeal.

More specifically, this one sentence formulation of the issue(s) in question form contains:

1) the key facts, or some of them

2) the particular element, or language, of either the cause-of-action or the defense about which there is a question on appeal

3) reference to the rule which requires the element.

Correct statements of the issue

An example of a statement of the issue in controversy in a one sentence question is:

-- Did A's being pushed against B in a crowded subway car during rush hour constitute an offensive touching by A as required for the intentional tort of battery?

This example illustrates the three components of an issue, as follows:

1) Key facts:	A was pushed against B in a crowded subway car during rush hour.
2) Particular element of battery:	An offensive touching
3) Reference to the applicable rule:	Intentional tort of battery.

Another example of a statement of the issue in controversy is:

-- Did A have the requisite intent to burn a structure as required for arson when, while burning leaves in his backyard, a tornado suddenly appeared, spread A's fire to ten nearby houses and destroyed them?

The three parts of this issue could be identified as follows:

1) Key facts:	Sudden tornado spread A's leaf-burning fire in his backyard to ten nearby houses and destroyed them.

2) Particular element of arson: Intent to burn a structure.

3) Reference to the applicable rule: Arson.

Incorrect statements of the issue

One way to appreciate correct formulations of an issue is to understand exactly why incorrect formulations are wrong. The following two formulations are incorrect:

-- Is the defendant liable for the intentional tort of battery?

-- Is A liable for arson?

The common vice in both formulations of the issue is that they fail to incorporate any key facts. All three inquire about liability in the form of pure legal conclusions. All cases, however, determine liability about particular facts. There is no issue and no liability without such facts. This is expressed well by an Iowa court:

> It is almost a legal maxim that out of the facts the law arises, since, if there be no state of facts, there can be no question of law.

Hence, a formulation of an issue must include at least some of the key facts.

Examples of another type of incorrect formulation of issues follows.

-- Was A pushed against B in the crowded subway car during rush hour?

-- Was A's leaf-burning fire in his backyard spread by the sudden tornado to ten nearby houses destroying them?

The common defect in these two formulations of the issue is that they are purely factual. They fail to raise a question about the legal significance of these facts. Cases, however, not only inquire about facts. They also inquire about their legal significance. Hence, a formulation of an issue must also raise a question about liability (e.g., for battery; for arson; for breach of contract).

Hints for formulating issues

First, most first-year professors want you to be quite specific in framing issues. One reason is that courts, contrary to what some beginning students believe, ordinarily decide cases on the narrowest ground (issue) presented by the facts. Often the narrowest ground is a procedural issue. Courts do not imitate Zeus in hurling thunderbolts from

Mount Olympus. Many of your professors therefore insist on narrow framings of issues.

Second, sometimes courts in opinions specify which issues are not presented by the case. This negative formulation can help you to zero in on the issue(s) which is raised.

Third, it makes sense as you meticulously read to search for an explicit statement by the court of the issue presented in the case. Explicitly stated issues are often plainly expressed: "the issue presented is whether...."; or "the question in this case is whether...."; or comparable language. Sometimes the issue is implicit, not explicit; or an explicitly stated issue may be stated imprecisely or even incorrectly. In these situations, you must extricate the issue from the case. Examples follow in this and later chapters.

Holding

If the issue in controversy poses the question which must be resolved to decide the appeal, the holding is the court's resolution, the answer to that question. Thus, the guidelines for determining the holding are simple.

> Two Guidelines for Determining Holdings
>
> 1) Identify the issue in controversy in the appellate court opinion.
>
> 2) Identify the holding by extricating the answer to this issue.

The holding is usually one sentence, a declarative sentence which identifies:

1) the key facts or some of them

2) the particular element, or language, of the rule (either the cause-of-action or the defense) which presents the crux of the dispute on appeal

3) the rule which requires the element.

Correct statement of holdings

An example of a correct statement of a holding is:

-- A's being pushed against B in a crowded subway during rush hour was not an offensive touching by A as required for the intentional tort of battery.

The breakdown of this holding into its three constituent parts is identical with the previous breakdown for the related issue into three parts (see p. 28). The only difference between the statement of the issue and the statement of the holding is that the issue is in the form of a question and the holding is in the form of a declarative sentence.

Another example of a correct statement of a holding is:

-- A did not have the intent to burn a structure as required for arson when a tornado suddenly appeared and spread A's leaf-burning fire in his backyard to ten nearby houses and destroyed them.

This holding, too, can be broken down into the identical three parts as can the statement of the related issue. Identify these three parts (see p. 28).

Incorrect statements of holdings

Incorrect statements of holdings parallel incorrect statements of issues. For example:

-- The defendant is liable for the intentional tort of battery (see p. 29).

-- A is not liable for arson (see p. 29).

Again, the vice is that these holdings contain no facts. They are pure legal conclusions (see p. 29).

You should be able to determine the weakness in the following holdings.

-- A was pushed against B in the crowded subway car during rush hour.

-- A's leaf-burning fire in his backyard was spread to ten nearby houses destroying them.

Again, the defect here is that these holdings are purely factual (see p. 29).

Hints for determining holdings

Just as you searched the opinion for an explicit statement of the issue, you must also search for an explicit statement of the holding: "the holding is..."; or "we hold..."; or sometimes "we conclude..." or "we find..." Be careful, the latter two statements are often not the holding but rather a conclusion in the reasoning or a factual conclusion.

As in issue-spotting, sometimes the holding is implicit rather than explicit. In these situations, you must extricate the holding from the case. Sometimes, too, the explicit holding by the court is cryptic, imprecise, or even incorrect. Here, again, you must extricate the correct holding. Examples of implicit and incorrect holdings follow in this and later chapters.

Judgment

The judgment is the disposition of the appellate case you are briefing. It's also called the result. In the language of systems analysis, it's the output of the case. In the vernacular, the judgment announces who won what and who lost what. It should always be distinguished from the holding of the case. While the judgment may be mentioned early in an appellate opinion, the judgment is almost always specified at the end of the opinion and is therefore easy to identify.

> Three Guidelines for Determining Judgments
>
> 1) Identify judgment of trial court.
> 2) Identify judgment of intermediate appellate court.
> 3) Identify judgment of appellate case which you are briefing.

1. Identify the trial court's judgment. Who won what in the trial court. You have already accomplished this step in determining the procedural history of the case (see pp. 25-6).

2. Identify the judgment of the intermediate appellate court, if there was intermediate appellate court review. Does this judgment affirm, reverse, or modify the trial court's judgement? Again, you have already accomplished this step in figuring out the procedural history (see p. 26).

3. Lastly, identify the judgment of the current appellate court, almost always located at the end of the opinion -- e.g., judgment for plaintiff affirmed; or judgment for defendant reversed.

If there was no intermediate appellate court review, the judgment referred to is the trial court judgment. Remember that in many states there is no intermediate appellate court. Remember too that in many instances the opinion you are briefing is an opinion of an intermediate appellate court. If, however, there was an intermediate appellate court opinion, and the current judgment is by the highest appellate court in a state (often called the supreme court), then the judgment of such court will affirm, reverse, or modify the judgment of the intermediate appellate court (see Judgment, pp. 55-6).

Reasoning

After briefing the facts, procedural history, issue, holding and judgment, you are ready to dissect the reasoning: the court's explanation and justification for its holding, its resolution of the issue in controversy. While courts need not explain and justify their holdings, there is a powerful tradition which usually leads to such explanation and justification by appellate courts. A court's decision (its holding and judgment) is supposed to be rationalized by an appeal to precedent, principle or policy rooted in a repertoire of traditionally acceptable types of legal argument, and not an expression of arbitrariness, mere power, or bias. The court's reasoning is an effort to demonstrate that its decision is justified by precedent, principle or policy. This reasoning is scrutinized by judges and lawyers who may apply it in future cases.

Three Guidelines for Understanding the Reasoning

1) Identify the separate arguments.

2) Identify the types of argument applied by the court.

3) Appreciate the varying weight of different arguments.

1. Identify the arguments.

Initially, you must distinguish the reasoning from the holding. Sometimes, this distinction is clear. The court's holding is explicitly stated ("we hold...." or "we decide....") and is not cryptic, imprecise or incorrect; and its reasons are clearly an explanation and justification for its holding. Sometimes, however, the distinction is not so clear. If, for example, the holding is implicit in the court's reasoning, the holding must be extricated from the reasoning and different judges and opposing lawyers may extricate the holding in somewhat different formulations (see pp. 31-2).

After separating the holding from the reasons for the holding, you must identify the separate reasons or arguments. Hypothesize that there is probably more than one reason embodied in the court's explanation and justification. What is the basis for this hypothesizing? Experience.

Most of the appellate cases you'll study will have two or more such reasons.

Be aware, however, that appellate courts do not always specify reasons. The facts may be so compelling, the applicable rule so well established, that there is simply no need to explain and justify the obvious.

2. <u>Identify the types of argument</u>.

Learning the law includes learning the repertoire of traditionally acceptable types of legal arguments applied by appellate courts in their reasoning. Where are these types of legal arguments found? A simple, but not simplistic, response is that these types of reasons or arguments are entrenched in the case law, in thousands of cases. Your first-year subjects, including contracts, torts, criminal law and property, are history-packed areas of law. The reasons applied by courts are rooted mostly in the vast case law in each area which has emerged over decades and even centuries. Each new case is like a new wave from the ocean: it has been preceded by countless prior waves. It is new but the process is old. Thus, learning each first-year subject includes learning, mostly from the case law, the particular repertoire of traditionally acceptable types of reasoning for that subject -- for contracts, torts, criminal law, property, etc. While it is beyond the scope of this book to set forth the particular repertoires for each first-year subject, identifying this task for you may shed light on what is expected.

The general repertoire of traditionally acceptable types of reasoning is vast. It includes the following:

A) arguments based on precedent

B) arguments designed to show a compelling need for the decision in the facts (factual arguments)

C) claims of fairness or justice which require the decision

D) claims of utility or pragmatism for the majority or for a large number of people whose economic, political or social well-being will be enhanced by the decision

E) claims of legal principle(s) which warrants the decision (overlapping with A, C and D)

F) claims of policy purpose(s) or interest(s) of the law, which justifies the decision, a vast arena of argument which overlaps with A, C, D and E

G) claims of logic, including avoidance of non-sequiturs, contradictions and inconsistencies, which crosscut and underpin all of the above arguments and which justify the decision

If you're looking for precise categories, clear definitions and consistent language, disappointment is your destiny. What one judge calls a policy may be described by another as a principle (or doctrine). Arguments explicitly of a factual or logical character often mask hidden policy assumptions. Claims of justice and utilitarian benefit are often confused and contradictory. In contrast, the reasoning in some opinions rings with clarity, insight and persuasiveness: it is compelling.

What your professors demand is that you gradually become familiar with this vast repertoire of types of legal reasoning in their concrete exemplification in cases in each subject, and that you manifest skill in class and on exams by justifying your legal position-taking with appropriate use of such arguments. To be comfortable in class and to do well on exams (and in practice), you must sharpen your skill in identifying, categorizing, succinctly presenting and understanding the types of arguments used to justify decisions in each subject. One warning: your professors expect concreteness in identifying and applying such arguments. It's not a matter of mentioning magic general words, say of principle or policy, that counts. Rather, you must identify the particular principle or policy which applies in a case.

Interpreting a statutory rule

While the repertoire of argument is vast, it's not without rhyme or reason. Depending on the type of issue and holding in a particular case, some arguments are available, some are not. First, if you have identified the issue and holding, you may have identified a dispute over the meaning of a statutory rule, or element of such a rule, as the crux of an opinion. The McBoyle case set forth later in this chapter is an example of this common type of case. Once you know that interpretation of a statutory rule, or element, is the issue in controversy, you'll learn in this chapter that a particular set of arguments relating mainly to determining the intention of the legislature is applicable. Some of these arguments are detailed later in this chapter by Justice Holmes in the McBoyle case.

Applying a judge-made rule

Second, if your briefing of the facts, issue and holding reveals instead that a case-based rule, not a statute, presents the issue in controversy, you'll learn in chapters III through V that a variety of different kinds of argument is applicable in the reasoning. The exact kinds of argument which are applicable depend on the subject and the specific case rule and facts at stake. For example, the arguments applied in the Woods case set forth in Chapter V are quite different from the arguments set forth in Sauer and Greaves in Chapter IV and from the arguments set forth in Port Huron in Chapter III. Nevertheless, all these cases, except Woods, present a typical focus found in many cases:

the issue in controversy centers on whether or not one or two specific elements in a judge-made rule were established by the facts presented in the case.

For example, the controversy in Port Huron centered on whether or not the facts established the element of acceptance necessary for a contract (offer, acceptance, consideration). In Sauer and Greaves, the controversy centered on whether or not the facts established a breach of the standard of reasonable care necessary for a negligent tort (duty, standard of care, breach, factual and legal causation, and actual harm). The factual and policy arguments in the reasoning in Sauer and Greaves pinpointed this specific dispute. The controversy in these cases did not center on other elements. The specific arguments utilized illustrate how the reasoning in a case can help you to zero in on exactly what is at issue and exactly what is not at issue. See the specific arguments used in the reasoning in a case not as peculiar to that case but as concrete application of types of reasoning deeply embedded in our law. Learn to apply these arguments in each subject.

3. Appreciate the varying weight of arguments.

Gradually, you can begin to appreciate that not all reasons or arguments in appellate opinions are intended to be of equal importance. Do not assume that if two, four, or six reasons are set forth that the court intends each to be of equal weight. Instead, hypothesize to the contrary and ask yourself -- which of these arguments seems to be most important. Look for words indicating weight, including "it is important..." or "what is decisive...." Look too for weight as manifested in the amount of space devoted to each argument.

Let your professor be your guide. Which arguments are stressed by your professor in class? Which are treated as secondary? Which are ignored? If your professor stresses one argument, she or he may intend to teach you about that one argument with that case. The other arguments in the case may not be important at the moment because of your professor's pedagogical strategy. Try to go with the flow of her pedagogic strategy. It will go easier for you in class and on exams.

Dicta

Dicta (dictum - singular) means discussion in an opinion which is not necessary to the holding. If you recall that a holding is the answer to the issue in controversy, the issue which must be decided to resolve the controversy presented in the case, you have a criterion for determining whether specific aspects of the opinion are dicta. If the discussion seems incidental to the holding, it may well be dicta.

Sometimes, dicta in an opinion is plainly identifiable. The court may discuss an issue which is not the issue in controversy. Occasionally, such dicta may even be acknowledged (e.g., "an issue not presented here is..." or "this appeal does not raise the issue..."). Occasionally, too, judges in an opinion may discuss an opinion which is clearly not on point with the facts and issue in the current appeal. Another example of clear dicta is presented in Port Huron set forth in Chapter III. The court's opinion offered a pedagogic review, among other things, of basic rules of contract law, much of which was unnecessary for the court's decision of the appeal.

Alas, not all examples of dicta are plainly identifiable. What one judge believes to have been necessary to a holding, another judge may classify as incidental. What one judge may label as dicta, another judge may label as part of the policy discussion or part of the presentation of the underlying principle of the case (see p. 75) or of its ratio decidendi (see p. 75). The best way to increase your skill in identifying dicta is to observe how judges in opinions classify certain arguments as dicta and to listen closely to your professor's comments on dicta in each course.

A Caveat on the Guidelines

Do not expect to be able to apply these guidelines mechanically in every case you brief. The cases are too varied, the facts and issues too diverse, to permit invariable, mechanical application. For example, the issue in controversy in the Woods case presented in Chapter V concerns an entire rule, rather than an element or two of a rule. This variety and diversity does not invalidate the guideline approach; rather, it requires modification which is illustrated later.

IV. APPLICATION OF GUIDELINES

Let's apply the approach to briefing specified above to a simple, short case decided by the United States Supreme Court. Scan McBoyle v. United States quickly in a first reading and then read it meticulously at least two or three times. Then brief the case applying the guidelines set forth above. Do this systematically, beginning with the guidelines for extricating the key facts, and so on. Use the steps suggested previously: Facts, Procedural History, Issue, Holding, Judgment, Reasoning (see pp. 21-2).

McBOYLE *v.* UNITED STATES.

CERTIORARI TO THE CIRCUIT COURT OF APPEALS FOR THE TENTH CIRCUIT.

No. 552. Argued February 26, 27, 1931.—Decided March 9, 1931.

***

CERTIORARI, 282 U. S. 835, to review a judgment affirming a conviction under the Motor Vehicle Theft Act.

Mr. Harry F. Brown for petitioner.

Mr. Claude R. Branch, Special Assistant to the Attorney General, with whom *Solicitor General Thacher, Assistant Attorney General Dodds* and *Messrs. Harry S. Ridgely* and *W. Marvin Smith* were on the brief, for the United States.

MR. JUSTICE HOLMES delivered the opinion of the Court.

The petitioner was convicted of transporting from Ottawa, Illinois, to Guymon, Oklahoma, an airplane that he knew to have been stolen, and was sentenced to serve three years' imprisonment and to pay a fine of $2,000. The judgment was affirmed by the Circuit Court of Appeals for the Tenth Circuit. 43 F. (2d) 273. A writ of certiorari was granted by this Court on the question whether the National Motor Vehicle Theft Act applies to aircraft.

Act of October 29, 1919, c. 89, 41 Stat. 324; U. S. Code, Title 18, § 408. That Act provides: "Sec. 2. That when used in this Act: (a) The term 'motor vehicle' shall include an automobile, automobile truck, automobile wagon, motor cycle, or any other self-propelled vehicle not designed for running on rails; . . . Sec. 3. That whoever shall transport or cause to be transported in interstate or foreign commerce a motor vehicle, knowing the same to have been stolen, shall be punished by a fine of not more than $5,000, or by imprisonment of not more than five years, or both."

Section 2 defines the motor vehicles of which the transportation in interstate commerce is punished in § 3. The question is the meaning of the word 'vehicle' in the phrase "any other self-propelled vehicle not designed for running on rails." No doubt etymologically it is possible to use the word to signify a conveyance working on land, water or air, and sometimes legislation extends the use in that direction, e. g., land and air, water being separately provided for, in the Tariff Act, September 22, 1922, c. 356, § 401 (b), 42 Stat. 858, 948. But in everyday speech 'vehicle' calls up the picture of a thing moving on land. Thus in Rev. Stats. § 4, intended, the Government suggests, rather to enlarge than to restrict the definition, vehicle includes every contrivance capable of being used "as a means of transportation on land." And this is repeated, expressly excluding aircraft, in the Tariff Act, June 17, 1930, c. 997, § 401 (b); 46 Stat. 590, 708. So here, the phrase under discussion calls up the popular picture. For after including automobile truck, automobile wagon and motor cycle, the words "any other self-propelled vehicle not designed for running on rails" still indicate that a vehicle in the popular sense, that is a vehicle running on land, is the theme. It is a vehicle that runs, not something, not commonly called a vehicle, that flies. Airplanes were well known in 1919, when this statute was passed; but it is admitted that they were not mentioned in the reports or in the debates in Congress.

It is impossible to read words that so carefully enumerate the different forms of motor vehicles and have no reference of any kind to aircraft, as including airplanes under a term that usage more and more precisely confines to a different class. The counsel for the petitioner have shown that the phraseology of the statute as to motor vehicles follows that of earlier statutes of Connecticut, Delaware, Ohio, Michigan and Missouri, not to mention the late Regulations of Traffic for the District of Columbia, Title 6, c. 9, § 242, none of which can be supposed to leave the earth.

Although it is not likely that a criminal will carefully consider the text of the law before he murders or steals, it is reasonable that a fair warning should be given to the world in language that the common world will understand, of what the law intends to do if a certain line is passed. To make the warning fair, so far as possible the line should be clear. When a rule of conduct is laid down in words that evoke in the common mind only the picture of vehicles moving on land, the statute should not be extended to aircraft, simply because it may seem to us that a similar policy applies, or upon the speculation that, if the legislature had thought of it, very likely broader words would have been used. *United States* v. *Thind,* 261 U. S. 204, 209.

Judgment reversed.

Facts

1. By applying the first guideline -- identification of the parties and their roles (see p. 23) -- you identify that at trial the government was the plaintiff and McBoyle was the defendant.

2. By applying the second guideline -- identification of plaintiff's cause-of-action and its elements (see p. 24) -- you identify a federal crime, Section 3 of the National Motor Vehicle Theft Act, as the government's cause-of-action against McBoyle at trial. You next identify the elements of this cause-of-action:

A) whoever

B) transports (or causes to be transported)

C) in interstate (or foreign) commerce

D) a motor vehicle

E) knowing it to have been stolen -- is liable.

3. By applying the third guideline -- identification of the element(s) of the cause-of-action, which poses the conflict on appeal (see p. 24) -- you identify element D above as the element which seems to pose the conflict on this appeal. You should specify, as the Court did, the definition of "motor vehicle" set forth in Section 2 of the Act: "...an automobile, automobile truck, automobile wagon, motor cycle, or any other self-propelled vehicle not designed for running on rails."

4. By applying the fourth guideline -- identification of facts most relevant to the element(s) which poses the conflict on appeal (see p. 24) -- you identify the facts which seem most relevant to this element. In this case, the facts are simple, short and are set forth in conclusory form at the beginning of the opinion:

> McBoyle was convicted of violating the National Motor Vehicle Theft Act by transporting from Illinois to Oklahoma an airplane he knew to have been stolen.

5.&6. With respect to the fifth and sixth guidelines -- identification of any defense and its element(s) in question on appeal and the facts most relevant to this element(s) (see p. 24) -- it is unnecessary to apply these guidelines in briefing McBoyle. Why? The Court's opinion does not stress a defense and, thus, the application of the first four guidelines is adequate here.

Hence, your statement of the facts might be as follows:

Facts

McBoyle v. U.S.
283 U.S. 25 (1931)

The petit. on appeal, McBoyle, was prosecuted by the fed. govern. and convicted at trial of violating the Nat. Motor Veh. Theft Act for transporting an airplane from Ill. to Okla., knowing plane to have been stolen.

That Act (Sec. 3) specifies that
A) whoever
B) transports (or causes to be transported)
C) in interstate (or foreign) commerce
D) a motor vehicle
E) knowing it to have been stolen
-- is liable.

Section 2 of Act defines motor vehicle as "automobile, auto truck, auto wagon, motor cycle or any other self-propelled vehicle not designed for running on rails."

Procedural History

1.2.&3. By extricating the key facts, you have already identified the information sought in these three guidelines -- parties, cause-of-action, and disposition by trial court (see pp. 25-6).

4.&5. By applying these guidelines -- identification of appealing party and court, relief requested and any disposition by intermediate appellate court (see p. 26) -- you identify that McBoyle is the petitioner in the United States Supreme Court. He has been granted a writ of certiorari to appeal to the Supreme Court. He seeks reversal of the affirmance by the U.S. Court of Appeals (10th Cir.) of the trial court's judgment of conviction for violating Section 3 of the National Motor Vehicle Theft Act. The U.S. Court of Appeals is the federal, intermediate appellate court (see p. 6).

Hence, your abbreviated statement of the procedural history might read:

Procedural History

Judg. of convict. of McBoyle by trial ct. of Sec. 3 of Act affirmed by U.S. Ct. of Appeals (10th Cir.) & U.S. Sup. Ct. granted writ of certiorari.

Issue

1.2.&3. You have already identified the information sought in these three guidelines -- identification of cause-of-action at trial and its element(s); the element(s) of the cause-of-action which poses the conflict on appeal; and the appellate court's marshalling of the facts (see p. 27).

4. It is unnecessary to apply the fourth guideline -- which is repeating guidelines 1-3 applied to any defense emphasized by the court (see p. 27).

5. Applying this guideline -- a one sentence formulation of the issue(s) in controversy (see pp. 28-30) -- there are two explicit issue statements suggested in Justice Holmes' Supreme Court opinion:

A) the issue is whether the National Motor Vehicle Theft Act applies to aircraft?

B) the issue is whether the meaning of the word "vehicle" specified in part of Section 2 of the National Motor Vehicle Theft Act -- "any other self-propelled vehicle not designed for running on rails" -- applies to aircraft?

The second formulation of the issue is superior. Why? It precisely identifies the issue in controversy to be decided by the appellate court. Remember that most first-year professors want you to be specific in framing issues (see pp. 29-30). Understand how this second formulation of the issue in controversy fulfills the three parts of a good statement of the issue:

1)	Key fact:	Aircraft
2)	Particular element or language:	Part of Section 2 of Act: "...any other self-propelled vehicle not designed for running on rails."
3)	Reference to the rule:	National Motor Vehicle Theft Act

Notice in B) above that the issue is not focused generally on the definition of a motor vehicle set forth in Section 2 of the Act. Instead, it pinpoints the precise language within that section which raises the issue in controversy.

This is the reason why the second formulation of the issue is superior. The first formulation fails to pinpoint the precise language at stake and therefore fails to distinguish between this language and other language in Section 2 which does not raise the issue in controversy. For example, an aircraft is plainly not a "motor cycle" and not an "automobile truck." No issue is raised by this latter language.

Making these distinctions requires that you understand that one purpose in briefing appellate cases is to pinpoint the exact issue in controversy in order to pinpoint the exact holding. Making these distinctions requires meticulous, lawyerly reading of the opinions. You must read like a lawyer in order to think, talk and write like a lawyer.

Overbroad Statements of Issues

With this insight, the defect in the following formulation of the issue should be apparent:

> the issue is whether in federal law the word "vehicle" applies to aircraft.

This formulation is manifestly wrong on its face because it is far too broad: the case deals only with certain words in Section 2 of the National Motor Vehicle Theft Act, not with federal law in a sweeping sense. This mistake overlooks what is central. Courts in deciding cases resolve only the issue in controversy: the question which is posed by the facts considered in light of an applicable rule, an element of that rule and, as here, certain language of that element set forth in Section 2 of the Act. Nothing else is decided. What is illustrated here is that our courts proceed case by case, step by step, with intense concern for the limited facts presented in a case.

The vice in the following formulation of the issue may also be apparent to you:

> -- the issue is whether it is unconstitutional to apply the word "vehicle" in Section 2 of the National Motor Vehicle Theft Act to aircraft?

The vice here results from failure to read like a lawyer (meticulously) and reflects a beginner's blunder of inserting into a case what is not there: a constitutional issue.

Holding

1.&2. By applying these two guidelines -- identifying the question in issue and the answer to that question (see p. 30) -- you extract the answer given by the appellate court. Once you have pinpointed the issue in controversy, identifying the holding should be easy. You change the issue in controversy embodied in a question into a declarative sentence. Here, for example:

> -- The holding is that the meaning of the word "vehicle" specified in part of Section 2 of the Nat. Motor Veh. Theft Act -- "any other self-propelled vehicle not designed for running on rails" -- does not apply to aircraft.

Notice that, like the statement of the issue, this statement of the holding is divisible into three constituent parts: 1) key facts; 2) particular element, or language; and 3) a reference to the rule (see

p. 30). Notice, too, as in many appellate cases, the opinion in McBoyle does not explicitly state the holding. There are no magic words here denoting the holding (e.g., "we hold" or "we decide"). Nevertheless, because you have identified the precise issue in controversy, you can extract the holding.

Overbroad Statements of Holdings

You should be able to appreciate that the following statement of the holding is less precise because it fails to specify what words in Section 2 of the Act make Section 3 of the Act inapplicable to aircraft.

> The holding is that Section 2 of the National Motor Vehicle Theft Act does not apply to aircraft.

What are the vices in the following statements of the holding?

> 1) The holding is that it is unconstitutional to apply the word "vehicle" to aircraft.
>
> 2) The holding is that in federal law the word "vehicle" does not apply to aircraft.

The first holding is plainly erroneous. The second holding is a virtual model of overbreadth, of what a holding is not. In legal reasoning, it is a classic beginner's blunder. The case does not deal with the global abstraction of "federal law." Not at all. It deals, as noted, only with certain words in Section 2 of the National Motor Vehicle Theft Act. Beware of articulating holdings in the form of sweeping generalizations. They are wrong. They violate a cardinal premise of legal reasoning: holdings are fact-bound, fact-limited, intended to apply only to a limited range of fact situations.

Judgment

1.&2. You have already identified the information sought by these two guidelines -- the judgment of the trial court and of any intermediate appellate court (see p. 32) -- in determining the procedural history of McBoyle (see p. 42). You know that there was a judgment of conviction of McBoyle at trial for violation of Section 3 of the National Motor Vehicle Theft Act. You know too that the intermediate federal appellate court, the United States Court of Appeals (10th Circuit), affirmed this trial court judgment of conviction.

3. By applying this guideline -- identification of judgment of appellate opinion which you are briefing (see p. 32) -- you identify the judgment of the current appellate court, the United States Supreme Court, at the end of the opinion:

> Judgment reversed.

These words, however, are too cryptic for your purposes. You must specify their meaning. For example:

The judgment of the United States Court of Appeals (10th Cir.), affirming the trial court judgment of conviction of McBoyle, is reversed. (The effect of this reversal is to overturn the trial court judgment of conviction.)

Reasoning

1. By applying this guideline -- identifying the separate legal arguments (see pp. 33-4) -- you first distinguish the holding from the reasons, and you identify and number the reasons or arguments. Since you know the holding, distinguishing it from the reasons is possible. Your identification and numbering of the reasons might look like the following.

A) In everyday, popular usage, the meaning of vehicle and airplane is different. A vehicle runs on land; an airplane flies.

B) State statutes (e.g., Conn., Ohio & Michigan), and weight of federal statutes (e.g., Tariff Act of 1930), agree with popular usage.

C) No evidence of congressional intent to include aircraft when this statute was passed in 1919 -- no mention in committee reports or in congressional debate (though airplanes were well known in 1919).

D) Holding serves objective that criminal statutes give fair warning of penalty if "a certain line is passed." Fairness requires a "clear" line.

E) Holding serves objective of judicial restraint. Court will not extend the statute because the policy served is identical in punishing the transportation of either a stolen vehicle or a stolen aircraft in interstate commerce; or because Congress may simply have forgotten planes and would "very likely" have used "broader words" if it had thought of the matter.

Don't be discouraged if you missed some of these arguments or did not distinguish among them. Separating arguments is difficult in the beginning. It presupposes knowledge which you do not yet have. Gradually, as you practice and know more, you'll see the separate arguments.

2. Applying the second guideline -- identifying the types of argument applied by the court (see pp. 34-6) -- is extremely difficult in the beginning because you do not have knowledge of these specific types of argument in each subject. Nevertheless, you must begin to practice.

From what has been said in explaining this guideline (see pp. 34-6), you should be aware that McBoyle, as many cases, raised an issue about interpretation of a statute, or, more precisely, posed an issue about interpretation of particular language in an element of a statutory rule. A court's power with such issues is limited to determining the intention of the legislature, here the Congress which enacted the statute. To determine legislative intent, particular types of reasoning or argument are appropriate. Where do these types of reasoning or argument come from? From the case law, from the thousands of cases decided over centuries of the common law. Justice Holmes, speaking for the court in McBoyle, used a few arguments typical of these types of reasoning. Indeed, the first three arguments in the opinion were all designed to discern congressional intent. They were means to this end.

Discerning Congressional Intent in McBoyle

Holmes' first argument was that one way to determine what Congress intended in using the word "vehicle" in Section 2 of the Act was to examine the every day, popular meaning of the word vehicle. Holmes concluded quickly that in this every day meaning a vehicle runs on land but not in the air.

Holmes' second argument was that another way to discern congressional intent is to examine other legislative use of the word "vehicle," both by Congress and by state legislatures. Holmes concluded that most of this use supports the Court's view. Incidentally, combining the first two arguments is fine, as long as you recognize the two parts of the argument.

Holmes' third argument was that congressional intent in this use of the word "vehicle" was revealed by congressional debate and committee reports when the statute was enacted in 1919. More exactly, Holmes' point here was that the absence of any mention of airplanes in such debate and reports in 1919, when airplanes were well known, supported the Court's view that Congress did not intend airplanes to be included in the definition of vehicle.

Notice how these three arguments designed to discern congressional intent were adroitly presented by Justice Holmes with each argument flowing into and supporting the other.

Policy Arguments in McBoyle

In addition to these three examples of specific types of reasoning or argument designed to determine legislative intent, the Court, speaking through Holmes, applied two policy arguments which are often applied when the issue presented is interpretation of a criminal statute.

The first policy argument applied was that fairness requires that criminal statutes give a clear and fair warning of what conduct is prohibited and of the penalty for violation. Holmes concluded that Section 2 of the Act gave no clear and fair warning that aircraft was covered.

The second policy argument applied was that courts, in interpreting criminal statutes, will not extend their meaning either to rectify legislative omissions or because the extension is desirable. The Congress should correct its own mistakes and omissions.

3. In applying the third guideline -- appreciating the varying weight of different arguments (see p. 36) -- it is difficult to determine which of the five arguments is more important. There are no explicit words signifying weight such as "it is important..." or "what is decisive...." More space is given to the first three arguments about legislative intent than to the last two policy arguments, but that does not seem decisive here. The conclusion is that the court clearly relied upon the two categories of arguments (relating to legislative intent and to specific policies) and it is not clear that the court weighted one over the other. Nevertheless, differences in weight given to these arguments by your professor might well vary from the Court's apparent weighting.

V. AN EXCELLENT BEGINNER'S BRIEF

Voilá, an excellent brief of McBoyle is a sum of the parts:

McBoyle v. U.S.
283 U.S.25 (1931)

Facts The petit. on appeal, McBoyle, was prosecuted by the Fed. Govern. and convicted at trial of violating the Nat. Motor Veh. Theft Act for transporting an airplane from Ill. to Okla., knowing plane to have been stolen.

That Act (Sec. 3) specifies that
- A) whoever
- B) transports (or causes to be transported)
- C) in interstate (or foreign) commerce
- D) a motor vehicle
- E) knowing it to have been stolen
  -- is liable.

Section 2 of Act defines motor vehicle as "automobile, auto truck, auto wagon, motor cyle or any other self-propelled vehicle not designed for running on rails."

Procedural History

Judg. of convic. of McBoyle by trial ct. of Sec. 3 of Act affirmed by U.S. Ct. of Appeals (10th Cir.) and U.S. Sup. Ct. granted writ of certiorari.

Issue Whether the meaning of the word "vehicle" specified in part of Section 2 of the National Motor Vehicle Theft Act -- "any other self-propelled vehicle not designed for running on rails" -- applies to aircraft?

Holding The meaning of the word "vehicle" specified in part of Section 2 of the Nat. Motor Veh. Theft Act -- "any other self-propelled vehicle not designed for running on rails" -- does not apply to aircraft.

Judgment

The judgment of the United States Court of Appeals (10th Cir.), affirming the trial court judgment of conviction of McBoyle, is reversed. (The effect of this reversal is to overturn the trial court judgment of conviction).

Reasoning

Determining Congressional Intent

1) In everyday, popular usage, the meaning of vehicle and airplane is different. A vehicle runs on land; an airplane flies.

2) State statutes (e.g., Conn., Ohio & Michigan), and weight of federal statutes (e.g., Traffic Act of 1930) agree with popular usage.

3) No evidence of congressional intent to include aircraft when this statute was passed in 1919 -- no mention in committee reports or in congressional debate (though airplanes were well known in 1919).

Policy

4) Holding serves objective that criminal statutes give fair warning of penalty if "a certain line is passed." Fairness requires a "clear" line.

5) Holding serves objective of judicial restraint. Court will not extend the statute because policy served is identical in punishing the transporting of either a stolen vehicle or a stolen aircraft in interstate commerce; or because Congress may simply have forgotten planes and would "very likely" have used "broader words" if it had thought of the matter.

VI. A POOR BRIEF

Contrast this excellent brief of McBoyle with a poor brief. My comments on the left specify weaknesses or refer you to a prior specification of weaknesses.

McBoyle v. U.S.
283 U.S. 25 (1931)

Comments	Facts
McBoyle was the defendant in trial court. Here on appeal,	The defendant, McBoyle, was convicted of violating the Nat.

he's described in the opinion as a petitioner. Use label of appellate court to avoid confusion.

Omission of statement of statutory rule violated (Sec. 3) and its elements and definition of "vehicle" (Sec. 2). This omission impedes pinpointing exactly what issue is in controversy on appeal.

Omits appeal to, and affirmance of judgment of conviction by, intermediate appellate court (U.S. Ct. of Appeals, 10th Cir.).

Wrong. Far too broad -- see pp. 29-30. Where does "aviation law" come from?

Wrong. Again, far too broad -- see pp. 30-1. Unsurprisingly, a wrong formulation of the issue leads to a wrong formulation of the holding.

Omits Judgment.

Mot. Veh. Theft Act. He transported an airplane from Ill. to Okla., knowing plane to be stolen.

<u>Procedural History</u>

McBoyle was convicted by trial court and now appeals to U.S. Sup. Ct.

<u>Issue</u>

The issue is whether in federal aviation law the word "vehicle" applies to aircraft?

<u>Holding</u>

The holding is that in federal aviation law the word "vehicle" does <u>not</u> apply to aircraft.

<u>Reasoning</u>

No doubt etymologically it is possible to use the word to signify a conveyance working on land, water or air, and sometimes legislation extends the use in that direction, e.g., land and air, water being separately provided for, in the Tariff Act, September 22, 1922. But in everyday speech "vehicle" calls up the picture of a thing moving on land. Thus in Rev. Stats. §4, intended, the government suggests, rather to enlarge

This merely repeats what is in opinion, virtually word for word. The objective, however, is not repetition but succinct ordering, categorizing and, hence, understanding.

than to restrict the definition, vehicle includes every contrivance capable of being used "as a means of transportation on land." And this is repeated, expressly excluding aircraft, in the Tariff Act, June 17, 1930. So here, the phrase under discussion calls up the popular picture. For after including automobile truck, automobile wagon and motor cycle, the words "any other self-propelled vehicle not designed for running on rails" still indicate that a vehicle in the popular sense, that is a vehicle running on land, is the theme. It is a vehicle that runs, not something, not commonly called a vehicle, that flies. Airplanes were well known in 1919, when this statute was passed; but it is admitted that they were not mentioned in the reports or in the debates in Congress. It is impossible to read words that so carefully enumerate the different forms of motor vehicles and have no reference of any kind to aircraft, as including airplanes under a term that usage more and more precisely confines to a different class. The counsel for the petitioner have shown that the phraseology of the statute as to motor vehicles follows that of earlier statutes of Connecticut, Delaware, Ohio, Michigan and Missouri, not to mention the late Regulations of Traffic for the District of Columbia, Title 6, c.9, §242, none of which can be supposed to leave the earth.

Although it is not likely that a criminal will carefully consider the text of the law before he murders or steals, it is reasonable that a fair warning should be given to the world in language that the common world will understand, of what the law intends to do if a certain line is passed. To make the warning fair, so far as possible the line should be clear. When a rule of conduct is laid down in words that evoke in the common mind only the picture of vehicles moving on land, the statute should not be extended to aircraft, simply because it may seem to us that a similar policy applies, or upon the speculation that, if the legislature had thought of it, very likely broader words would have been used. United States v. Thind, 261 U.S. 204, 209.

COMMENT

While Justice Holmes was a distinguished jurist in both the nineteenth and twentieth centuries, his reputation does not rest on his opinion for the Supreme Court in McBoyle. The point is not that McBoyle was wrongly decided or that Holmes' reasoning was atrocious. It was not. The point is that Holmes could have used other equally valid arguments from the repertoire of acceptable reasons to justify the opposite conclusion. While commentators speculate as to the Court's motivation in deciding McBoyle as it did, its motivation remains elusive. McBoyle illustrates what beginners do not know. A substantial segment of trial and appellate cases could be decided either way. In this segment of cases, a court's decision represents its best judgment on the facts and the applicable law. Another court might decide differently. The law is a human institution and hence the level of certainty in the law reflects inescapable human differences. Incidentally, it is illogical, and hence unlawyerly, to conclude, from the fact of uncertainty in decision-making in one segment of cases, that all decision-making in cases is uncertain.

VI. FUNCTIONS OF THE COURT EXEMPLIFIED IN McBOYLE

Interpreting Federal Statutes

1. Courts perform many functions in our legal system. A function performed by the United States Supreme Court in McBoyle is its role as the final judicial interpreter of federal statutes. Naturally, the trial judge also interprets applicable federal rules, both statutes and cases, necessary to decide a case. In addition, the intermediate appellate court, the United States Court of Appeals, interprets federal rules as required to decide appeals from judgments of federal trial courts

within its jurisdiction. The final arbiter, however, in deciding the interpretation of federal statutes is the United States Supreme Court. Here the United States Supreme Court is performing a function also carried out by the highest appellate court in each state, which is ordinarily the final arbiter of the meaning of its state statutes.

This above-explained function of the United States Supreme Court can also be expressed differently. In McBoyle, the Court's power, without a contitutional issue, is to discern the meaning of this congressional statute. The Court has no power to invalidate this statute because no constitutional issue is raised. The Federal Constitution authorizes Congress to enact statutes. In our governmental system of separation of powers, the power of the judiciary is to interpret the meaning of those statutes as applied in individual cases. Congress does not have judicial power to apply its statutes in individual cases. Hence, the issue for the Court is determining congressional intent in enacting Section 2 of this statute, not what the Court thinks the meaning should be.

Principled Decision-Making

2. In addition, the Court in McBoyle illustrates in its articulation of reasons a basic presupposition underlying all decision-making by courts at motion, trial and on appeal in our governmental system. Judicial decision-making is principled, meaning that it is rooted in legal reason and authority, and is not simply an exercise of personal power or power of office, whether mean-spirited or well intended. This presupposition gives concrete meaning to that primordial principle animating our legal system: ours is a rule of law, not persons. The existence of incompetent, lazy, biased or corrupt judges in no way denies the validity of that principle, which, incidentally, is also well served by many competent, conscientious, fair and honest judges.

VII. ISSUES NOT CONSIDERED AND DECIDED IN McBOYLE IN THE U. S. SUPREME COURT

One way to understand the particularity and discipline of legal reasoning in the case method is to identify the issues not considered and decided in McBoyle, and to understand why these issues were not considered and decided there. These include the following.

Issue	Answer
A) The issue is whether or not McBoyle knew the airplane was stolen?	Wrong: Resolved by the trial court.
B) The issue is whether or not McBoyle stole the aircraft?	Wrong: McBoyle is not charged with stealing the aircraft.

C) The issue is whether or not McBoyle transported an aircraft across state lines?

Wrong: Not the charge.

D) The issue is whether or not McBoyle transported (or caused to be transported) a motor vehicle in interstate commerce knowing it to be stolen?

Wrong: That was the correct issue at trial but not on appeal. Appellate courts review certain specific claims of legal error committed by trial courts. They do not simply rehash trial issues.

E) The issue is whether or not McBoyle was justly convicted?

Wrong: Claims of legal error to be reviewed by appellate courts are usually specific and not masked in vague references to justice.

F) The issue is whether or not the government's witnesses were credible?

Wrong: Resolved by the trial court.

G) The issue is whether or not McBoyle caused the plane to be transported in interstate commerce (i.e., across state lines) thereby giving the federal courts jurisdiction over the violation and over McBoyle?

Wrong: Resolved by the trial court and by the United States Court of Appeals for the Tenth Circuit.

H) The issue is whether or not the federal prosecutor proved McBoyle's legal guilt beyond a reasonable doubt?

Wrong: Resolved by the trial court.

I) The issue is whether or not McBoyle had a good motive or a bad motive for the violation?

Wrong: Motive is not a legal issue in determining McBoyle's liability.

J) The issue is whether or not the trial court conducted a careful investigation of all relevant factual and legal issues?

Wrong: Not the function of a common-law judge to conduct investigation.

K) The issue is whether or not a state court in interpreting state law is bound by the U.S. Supreme Court's interpretation in McBoyle?

Wrong: Not the function of the U.S. Supreme Court to decide interpretation of state law. State courts decide such interpretation.

This list of issues not considered and decided in McBoyle illustrates the central importance of distinguishing which issues are resolved at trial and which issues may be reviewed on appeal. Understanding this difference enables you to zero in on the issue(s) in controversy on appeal and hence to understand the holding. Many beginning law students are acutely confused because they do not distinguish between the broad range of issues which are decided by the trial court and the limited number of issues which are considered and decided on appeal.

VIII. A FEW MORE DEFINITIONS

Justice Holmes' opinion in McBoyle uses some legal terms, and presupposes others, which you should learn and which have not yet been defined. These include the following.

A) Petitioner. A petitioner is a person who initiates a petition which is a formal, written application to a court requesting judicial action on a specific matter. Here, McBoyle, acting though his lawyer, petitioned the Supreme Court to review the affirmance by the United States Court of Appeals (Tenth Circuit) of his judgment of conviction by the trial court.

B) Writ of Certiorari. Broadly, it is an order from a higher court (e.g., the United States Supreme Court) to an inferior court (e.g., the United States Court of Appeals) commanding the inferior court to produce the record of a trial for review by the higher court. Typically, it is a device used by the United States Supreme Court to decide which cases seeking review, as a matter of discretion, should be granted that review.

C) A Judgment. Broadly, a judgment is a final determination by a court of the issues presented to it in a proceeding. In McBoyle, Justice Holmes stated:

> The judgment was affirmed by the Circuit Court of Appeals for the Tenth Circuit.

This reference to judgment refers to the judgment of conviction by the trial court, meaning that McBoyle was determined by the trial court (judge and jury) to be liable for violation of Section 3 of the National Motor Vehicle Theft Act.

In addition, judgment is used again twice in McBoyle:

> Certiorari...to review a judgment affirming a conviction under the Motor Vehicle Theft Act.

This reference to judgment means the judgment of the United States Court of Appeals for the Tenth Circuit which affirmed the judgment of conviction of the federal trial court.

The last reference is at the end of the court's opinion:

Judgment Reversed

This means that the judgment of the United States Court of Appeals for the Tenth Circuit was overturned by the United States Supreme Court.

Beware of the one-word-one-meaning fallacy. Like many legal words, judgment has different applications. Be exact.

D) Decision. One of the many meanings of decision is the judgment of a court, at motion, trial or on appeal. Decision and judgment are sometimes used interchangeably by courts. Second, decision sometimes means the opinion of a court or its holding. Third, decision sometimes means a ruling or finding by a judge on a particular factual or legal issue during trial. Fourth, decision may mean a determination by a government agency or an administrative judge (e.g., after a Social Security hearing). As always, the specific context provides the particular meaning intended.

E) Intermediate Appellate Court. It is an appellate court (see prior definition, p. 6) which considers and decides appeals from specified trial courts but which is not the highest appellate court in a state or in the federal system. The United States Court of Appeals, organized into eleven circuits, is the intermediate appellate court in the federal court system. The United States Supreme Court is, of course, the highest appellate court in the federal court system. In the states, the names of the intermediate and highest appellate courts vary. In New York, for example, the highest appellate court is the New York State Court of Appeals; the intermediate appellate court is the Appellate Division; and the trial court of general jurisdiction is the New York State Supreme Court. In many states, however, the highest appellate court is called the Supreme Court -- e.g., the Supreme Court of California, the Supreme Court of Arkansas, the Supreme Court of Michigan; and the intermediate appellate court is often called the Court of Appeal(s). In addition, many states don't have an intermediate appellate court. Don't worry about learning all these names and forms of judicial organization at once. Gradually, you'll develop a sensitivity to these matters as you read cases from different states.

IX. WHAT'S THE MEANING OF ALL THESE ITEMS AT THE BEGINNING OF THE CASE?

Let's examine them item by item.

First, the caption of the case.

McBoyle v. United States

At the trial level, the order was reversed: the indictment by the federal jury read The United States v. McBoyle and that was the title of the trial proceeding because the federal government was prosecuting

McBoyle, not a private individual. Criminal prosecutions are carried out by the federal or state governments. Criminal law is public law, not private law. The parties are the state and the defendant, not the complainant (the victim) and the defendant. From our prior discussion, you may know why McBoyle's name goes first in the caption of the case. He was the petitioner in the United States Supreme Court; he had been granted a review by the Court of his claim of legal error committed by the United States Court of Appeals (10th Cir.). Another frequently used label to describe McBoyle's position is the "appellant."

Second, there is the citation:

283 U.S. 25 (1931)

This is the official citation for the McBoyle case in the United States Supreme Court. It means that this opinion is reported in Volume 283 of the United States Reports, the official, court-authorized system for reporting the cases decided by the Supreme Court. These cases are published by the Government Printing Office in Washington, D.C. The number "25" (283 U.S. 25) refers to the initial page on which the case is printed.

Third, there is the following:

No. 552 Argued February 26, 27, 1931 - Decided March 9, 1931

The "No. 552" refers simply to the Supreme Court docket number for this case, and the rest refers to the dates of oral argument by the lawyers before the Court and the official date of decision and publication of the opinion.

Fourth, there is the headnote:

> The National Motor Vehicle Theft Act, U.S.C., Title 18, re p. 39 §408, which punishes whoever transports, or causes to be transported, in interstate or foreign commerce a motor vehicle knowing it to have been stolen, and which defines "motor vehicle" as including "an automobile, automobile truck, automobile wagon, motor cycle, or any other self-propelled vehicle not designed for running on rails," does not apply to aircraft. P. 26.
>
> 43 F. (2d) 273, reversed.

I suggest scanning such headnotes but not concentrating on them. A headnote is a brief summary of the issues decided in a case, including the important facts. A headnote is not part of the court's opinion. It is added by the Reporter of Decisions or by the editor of the volume.

The citation, "43 F.(2d) 273, reversed," refers to the reversal by the Supreme Court of the judgment of the U.S. Court of Appeals (10th Cir.) which is reported in 43 F.2d 273, the forty-third volume of the Federal Reporter (an official system for reporting federal court cases other than Supreme Court cases) on page 273.

Fifth, beneath the headnote, you see the following:

CERTIORARI, 282 U.S. 835, to review a judgment affirming a conviction under the Motor Vehicle Theft Act.

You should be able to understand what this means. If not, please refer to my prior definition of the writ of certiorari (p. 55). The citation "282 U.S. 835" refers to the official report of the Supreme Court's decision on the preliminary proceeding by McBoyle asking the Court, in its discretion, to agree to hear and decide his claim of legal error. It reads:

> No. 552. McBoyle v. United States. January 12, 1931. Petition for writ of certiorari to the Circuit Court of Appeals for the Tenth Circuit granted, limited to the question whether the National Motor Vehicle Theft Act applies to aircraft. Mr. Harry F. Brown for petitioner, Solicitor General Thacher and Messrs. Claude R. Branch, Harry S. Ridgely, and W. Marvin Smith for the United States. Reported below: 43 F.(2d) 273.

Lastly, you see the following:

Mr. Harry F. Brown for Petitioner.

Mr. Claude R. Branch, Special Assistant to the Attorney General, with whom Solicitor General Thacher, Assistant Attorney General Dodds and Messrs. Harry S. Ridgely and W. Marvin Smith were on the brief, for the United States.

As may be apparent to you, Brown is the attorney who represented McBoyle in the Supreme Court. The other names refer to the government lawyers who represented the United States in the Supreme Court on this case.

While you concentrate in briefing and in class discussion on the court's opinion, you should be aware of the meaning of these preliminary matters.

I. INTRODUCTION

Applying what you have learned about briefing in the prior chapter, brief the following case in contracts. Use the six-step approach and apply the guidelines as demonstrated in the prior chapter. Two particular challenges are presented by this case.

First, you may have to struggle to understand the facts. As in many cases, they are somewhat complicated. For those of you with some business background, you may be able to understand the facts after two or three meticulous readings. For those many of you without such background, understanding these facts may require many meticulous readings, aided by Black's Law Dictionary and by Webster's English Dictionary. There is no escape from this effort: cases present fact situations from commerce and virtually every other area of life. Some fact patterns will be simple and clear as in <u>McBoyle</u>; many others will be complicated and unfamiliar, depending on your academic and work experience. One consolation: gradually you acquire an understanding of commercial and other fact patterns which initially may be quite strange. Remember, cases pivot on their facts: you must become fact-centered or, if you prefer, fact-obsessed.

Second, this court opinion includes varied types of legal reasoning. Your briefing challenge is to demonstrate that you understand the opinion by being able to identify, categorize, and succinctly present these varied types of legal reasoning. Your struggling to do so is a fundamental part of your learning of the basic skills.

Port Huron Machinery Company, Limited, Appellee, v. Fred Wohlers, Appellant.

***

Appeal from Des Moines Municipal Court.—**J. E. Mershon, Judge.**

November 13, 1928.

Rehearing Denied February 15, 1929.

Action at law, to recover liquidated damages, as stipulated in an alleged written contract or order for the purchase of certain farm machinery by the defendant (appellant) from the plaintiff. The defendant in answer admits that he signed the written order for purchase of the goods, and that he refused the shipment of the goods, but pleads an oral condition precedent, to wit: That the goods were to be delivered on or before a certain date, and that, by reason of his cancellation of the order before delivery, and before notification of acceptance of the order by plaintiff, an enforcible contract did not result. No evidence was introduced by the defendant. Upon the conclusion of the introduction of plaintiff's testimony, the defendant moved the court to instruct the jury to return a verdict for the defendant. This motion was overruled, and thereupon the plaintiff moved the court to instruct the jury to return a verdict for the plaintiff. This motion was sustained, and the jury was directed to return a verdict for the plaintiff in the sum of $349.55. Judgment was entered in conformity to the verdict, and the defendant appeals.—*Affirmed.*

Havens & Elston, for appellant.

Strock, Cunningham, Sloan & Herrick, for appellee.

De Graff, J.—This case involves an alleged contract containing a stipulation for liquidated damages. If a contract did result, there can be no question that the plaintiff is entitled to recover, since the terms of the alleged contract clearly fix the amount recoverable by plaintiff in case of a breach. See *Pace v. Zellmer*, 194 Iowa 516.

This appeal presents but one question. It is a question of law, and calls for the statement of the applicable legal principle. But, like every other case, the governing principle arises out of a fact situation. It is said in *Steffes v. Hale*, 204 Iowa 226:

> "It is almost a legal maxim that 'out of the facts the law arises,' since, if there be no state of facts, there can be no question of law."

We necessarily first turn to the factual side.

On July 18, 1927, a written order signed by the defendant was delivered to plaintiff's agent, and in that order the plaintiff was directed to deliver immediately, or as soon thereafter as possible, to the defendant on board cars, consigned to the order of plaintiff, at Neola, Iowa, defendant's place of residence, certain described goods (farm machinery). The order further states that the defendant will receive the machinery, pay the freight charges, and also pay to the plaintiff, on or before the arrival of the machinery, the sum of $1,562.50, in the manner and form recited in the order. Further:

> "If, for any reason, the purchaser fails to accept and settle for the machinery order, he will, if the company so elects and demands, pay to the company, in lieu of the enforcement of this contract, as liquidated damages, a sum equal to ten per cent of the list price, and, if shipment has been made, freight from the factory and return, demurrage, cartage, loading and unloading expense and all other similar expenses actually incurred by reason of the shipment and attempted delivery of said machinery; if suit is commenced to enforce the performance of any part of this contract the purchaser agrees to pay a reasonable attorney's fee."

The plaintiff's agent immediately, upon the signing of this order by defendant, telephoned the plaintiff at Des Moines the receipt of the order, and requested that the goods be loaded and sent forthwith to the defendant. On July 20, 1927, the plaintiff filled the order in accordance with its terms, and shipped the goods. On July 22, 1927, the plaintiff received a telegram from the defendant, bearing date July 21st, which said: "Delivery date specified on thresher deal now past and order is hereby cancelled." The plaintiff, as a result of defendant's attempt to revoke and cancel the order, and his refusal to accept the goods, was obliged to recall the goods and reship them to the point of delivery, thereby incurring certain expense, which was established by competent proof upon the trial of this case. True, the defendant in his answer alleged a condition precedent, but the allegation continued to rest in the answer. It finds no support in the evidence. When the plaintiff rested its case, motions for a directed verdict were made respectively by the parties. The plaintiff's motion was sustained. The question, therefore, at this point is whether the plaintiff established a prima-facie case. The contention of the defendant on appeal is that the plaintiff failed to prove a contract, for the reason that there is no showing that the plaintiff accepted the offer of the defendant and communicated the acceptance of the offer prior to its revocation by the defendant.

The point is now reached that we may discuss the law involved, under the undisputed facts. Did a contract result? It is not practicable, nor is it necessary, in a definition of contract, to state all of the operative facts or all of the legal relations that are created by such facts. A contract may be defined as a promise, the performance of which the law recognizes as a duty, and for a breach of which a remedy is given. A contract, therefore, does not contemplate simply the act of promising, but obligations arising therefrom. The law recognizes, as a matter of classification, two kinds of contracts,—unilateral and bilateral. In the case at bar, a typical example of unilateral contract is found, since it is universally agreed that a unilateral contract is one in which no promisor receives a promise as consideration; whereas, in a bilateral contract, there are mutual promises between the two parties to the contract. This matter of definition has recently received careful consideration by the American Law Institute, and may be found in the Restatement of the Law of Contracts, Proposed Final Draft No. 1 (April 18, 1928), 17, Section 12.

In the instant case, the offer of the defendant must be viewed as a promise. It is promissory in terms. The rule is well stated by Professor Williston: A promise which the promisor should reasonably expect to induce action or forbearance of a definite and substantial character on the part of the promisee, and which does induce such action or forbearance, is binding if injustice can be avoided only by enforcement of the promise. See 1 Williston on Contracts, Section 139. Clearly, the instant offer, signed by the defendant, was of this character. Appellant, however, contends that there was no acceptance of the offer. Words are not the only medium of expression of mutual assent. An offer may invite an acceptance to be made by merely an affirmative answer, or by performing a specific act. True, if an act other than a promise is requested, no contract exists until what is requested is performed or tendered, in whole or in part. We are here dealing with a unilateral contract, and the act requested and performed as consideration for the contract indicates acceptance, as well as furnishes the consideration. The sending of an order for goods to a merchant is an offer of a promise for an act. 13 Corpus Juris 266, Section 57. In the same text it is said that an acceptance of an offer may be by acts, as where an offer is made that the offerer will pay or do something else, if the offeree shall do a particular thing. In such a case, performance is the only thing needful to complete the agreement and to create a binding promise. Ibid. 275, Section 73. It must be kept in mind that there is a distinction in regard to communication of acceptance between offers which ask that the offeree *shall do* something, as in the instant case, and offers which ask that the offeree *shall promise* something. In offers of the latter kind, communication of the acceptance is always essential. Ibid. 284, 285, Sections 88, 89.

The decisions of this court are in accord with the general rule. In *Hankins v. Young*, 174 Iowa 383, it is said:

"In the case of an order for goods, the delivery of the goods in pursuance of the order is an acceptance of the order."

To the same effect is *Petroleum Prod. Distributing Co. v. Alton Tank Line,* 165 Iowa 398; *Rock Island Plow Co. v. Meredith,* 107 Iowa 498; *McCormick Harv. Mach. Co. v. Markert,* 107 Iowa 340. Pertinent language is used in *McCormick Harv. Mach. Co. v. Richardson,* 89 Iowa 525, wherein it is said:

"We do not say that the acceptance must be a formal one. The acceptance might be shown by proving an act done on the faith of the order, such as the shipment of the goods ordered."

An especially clear expression of the rule is found in *McDermott v. Mahoney,* 139 Iowa 292, wherein the written instrument was recognized and held to be a unilateral contract, as it was signed by one party only, and by him delivered to the other, and accepted as a contract between the parties. It is said:

"Where a written agreement signed by one party is accepted and adopted by the other, and acted upon, it becomes their contract, in the same sense as though both parties had signed it."

See, also, *Reynolds v. Johnson,* 199 Iowa 1055.

A typical case adopting the same rule is *Kingman & Co. v. Watson,* 97 Wis. 596 (73 N. W. 438). See, also, notes in 19 A. L. R. 476 and 29 A. L. R. 1352.

Certain cases are cited by appellant in brief, but they are distinguishable from the case at bar on the fact side. For instance: In *Thompson & Sons Mfg. Co. v. Perkins & Son,* 97 Iowa 607, the order was given in November, 1892, for goods to be shipped February 14, 1893. The offeree made no acceptance, either formal or by shipment, and, two weeks before shipment date, the offer was revoked. The revocation was held legally permissible, under the facts. The same is true in *Hargrove v. Crawford,* 159 Iowa 522; *Durkee v. Schultz,* 122 Iowa 410; *Doll & Smith v. A. & S. San. Dairy Co.,* 202 Iowa 786.

The instant appeal primarily has an educational value. The applicable legal principle is well settled, on both reason and authority. The judgment entered by the trial court is—*Affirmed.*

STEVENS, C. J., and ALBERT, MORLING, and WAGNER, JJ., concur.

III. AN EXCELLENT BEGINNER'S BRIEF

Contrast your brief with the following excellent brief. Language can vary, including method of expression and abbreviation. That is not critical. What is critical is to demonstrate a clear grasp of the facts, the procedural history, the precise issue in controversy, the holding and judgment, and an understanding of the reasoning. As you study this excellent brief, please reflect on my comments on the left.

PORT HURON MACH. CO., v. WOHLERS
207 Iowa 826 (1928)
221 NW 843

Comments

At trial, the seller was the plaintiff (P) and the buyer was the defendant (D). The appellate court used the same labels in its opinion. It helps to refer to the P-S (plaintiff-seller) and to the D-B (defendant-buyer). The case determined the rights and liabilities of a P-S and a D-B.

Note the step-by-step breakdown of the facts.

This segment specifies P-S's cause-of-action against D-B and elements of that c/a. This segment also specifies D-B's defense that no K existed because there was no acceptance. This statement of facts pinpoints element in controversy on appeal: the acceptance necessary for a K.

Facts

A) D-buyer delivered written order to P-seller's agent on 7/18/27 directing P to deliver farm machinery to D at Neola, Iowa.

B) The order also specified that if b/k by D-B, specified liquidated damages would be paid to P-S.

C) P-seller's A immed., upon receipt of signed order, called P-S at Des Moines & requested that machinery be loaded & sent to D-B. Shipped 7/20 per D-B's order to Neola, Iowa.

D) On 7/22, P-S received D-B's telegram: "Delivery date specified on thresher deal now past & order is hereby cancelled."

E) D-B refused shipment. P-S initiated c/a for money damages for b/k (offer, acceptance, consideration & breach). D-B argued on appeal that no K existed because P-S never accepted D-S's offer before D-S revoked his offer.

Procedural History

At end of P-S's case (i.e., the introduction of P-S's evidence) in trial court, both sides rested. D-B's motion for directed verdict for D-B rejected. P-S's motion for directed verdict for P-S granted for $349.55. Judgment entered for P-S. D-B appeals.

This statement of the procedural history pinpoints the exact disposition in the trial court and thus aids in pinpointing the issue in controversy to be resolved on appeal.

Issue

Whether the P-S's shipment of the machinery, as requested by D's order, constituted the acceptance necessary for a unilateral K?

A neutral, precise and hence preferable issue-formulation.

Holding

Yes. For a unilateral contract, acceptance of the offer was demonstrated by performance of the requested act -- here the shipping of the machinery. (No acceptance in the form of a promise was necessary.)

Again, this holding was implied or implicit, rather than being directly stated with words such as "we hold...."

Judgment

Judgment of trial ct. f/P-S affirmed.

The result or disposition here in the appellate court for the P-S affirmed the trial court result.

Reasoning

The court's reasoning is unusual because of its pedagogic style: a systematic presentation of the basic rules of contract law. Most court opinions are not comparably pedagogic on the convincing ground that cases are designed for decision of controversies, not for teaching law students. Hence, most, if not all, of this initial presentation of basic rules should be omitted, even though it is both true and fundamental, because it was not necessary to detail it to decide the appeal.

There was a unilateral K: an act was requested by D-B and performed by P-S; P's shipping of the machinery was both:

- acceptance &
- consideration

Corpus Juris (C.J.) is a legal encyclopedia, a comprehensive restatement in text form of American Law, topic by topic. Like the court's use of Professor Williston's analysis, Corpus Juris is another example of persuasive authority. Though often cited, it is not legally binding. Interweaving of key facts and elements of offer, acceptance & consideration necessary for a K.

As C.J. states: the sending of an order of goods to a merchant is an offer of a promise for an act. D's order was an offer and P's shipping of goods was acceptance and consideration. Performance, as here, completed the agreement and created a binding promise (a K).

There are two kinds of offers:

A) as here, P's offer asking D to do something (ship mach.)

B) an offer asking other party to promise something.

If latter, commun. of acceptance is essential.

In contrast to the persuasive authority of Professor Williston and Corpus Juris, the holdings of the court in its prior cases with similar facts and issues are binding authority; such holdings must be followed by the court in the instant case (see p. 7).

Ct. cites its prior decisions, Hawkins v. Young:

"In the case of an order for goods, the delivery of goods" per order "is an acceptance of order"; McDermott v. Mahoney: Where a written argument signed by 1 party is accept. and adopt. by other, and acted upon, it becomes their K. as though both parties had signed it.

The citation to a Wisconsin case and to the American Law Reports are additional examples of the Court's use of persuasive authority. The American Law Reports (ALR) is a digest of relevant cases, statutes and

Also in accord: a Wis. case and ALR

regulations, organized topic by topic.

The cases cited by the D-B in support of his defense were rejected by the court. Why? The facts in those cases were distinguishable, meaning they were not similar to the facts of this case. Hence, the holdings in those cases were not applicable here. They are precedents which did not control in this case.

Cases cited by appellant were factually distinguishable -- e.g., in Thompson v. Perkins, the offer (order) was never accepted (no shipment was made).

Comment

Did you notice that this brief is entitled An Excellent Beginner's Brief. Why? In the first few weeks of studying contracts, you are just learning the most basic rules of contracts. Hence, your detailing in the reasoning segment of your brief of some of these rules is justified; it helps you to learn them. After some weeks, however, there is no need for this detail even if the opinion contains it. Indeed, most opinions will short-circuit, or even presuppose, much of what the court here has specified. With experience and confidence, your reasoning segment could be presented as follows.

Reasoning

For a unilateral K., the performance of the act requested in an offer constitutes the acceptance. D-B's order was an offer and P-S's performance of act requested, shipment of farm machinery, was acceptance (& consideration). K results.

Authority

Binding: Ct.'s prior decisions:
Hawkins v. Young: "deliv. of goods" pursuant to an order is an "accept. of order."
Also in accord: McDermott v. Mahoney

Persuasive: Williston; C.J.; ALR

D's cases distinguishable on facts: no shipment made.

Remember: If K had been bilateral, then promise needed for acceptance.

The advantage of this more succinct recitation of the court's reasoning is not simply a saving of time. It is also a demonstration of focus: you pinpoint the heart of the reasoning -- the reason why your professor has assigned this case. Such pinpointing takes time -- and much briefing. (Incidentally, it is also possible here, with experience and confidence, to state the facts more succinctly).

Nevertheless, it's a mistake in the very beginning to attempt this degree of succinctness. Why? It presupposes what you do not have: the skills to pinpoint the essence of the reasoning. Hence, rather than being succinct, you risk being cryptic, missing important aspects of the reasoning.

IV. A POOR BRIEF

As you study this poor brief, your objectives are:

A) to understand exactly the defects in this brief and why these defects are wrong

B) to search for defects illustrated here which you are committing, and

C) hence, to avoid these mistakes.

Lacks date and citation

PORT HURON MACH. CO. v. WOHLERS

Comments

The mistakes here are:
A) the recitation of facts lacks concreteness
B) it does not specify who is the P and who is the D (the P-S and the D-B).

Facts

These facts relate to a sale of goods by seller to buyer. The seller apparently solicited the buyer to purchase the goods. The buyer placed an order with the seller to deliver the goods. Buyer agreed to pay $1562.50 for goods. Buyer's order also stated:

It's a mistake to quote extensively from the opinion. The errors of so doing are prolixity and a substitute for trying to identify and understand the key facts.

> "If, for any reason, the purchaser fails to accept and settle for the machinery order, he will, if the company so elects and demands, pay to the company, in lieu of the enforcement of this contract, as liquidated damages, a sum equal to ten per cent of the list price, and, if shipment has been made, freight from the factory and return, demurrage,

cartage, loading and unloading expense and all other similar expenses actually incurred by reason of the shipment and attempted delivery of said machinery; if the suit is commenced to enforce the performance of any part of this contract the purchaser agrees to pay a reasonable attorney' fee."

The order was shipped on July 20, 1927. The D, however, sent a telegram on 7/21, delivered on 7/22, cancelling his order:

> "Delivery date specified on thresher deal now past and order is hereby cancelled."

It's wrong to say D cancelled his order. It's correct to say D attempted to cancel his order.

P incurred costs in reshipping the goods.

> "True, the defendant in his answer alleged a condition precedent, but the allegation continued to rest in the answer. It finds no support in the evidence. When the plaintiff rested its case, motions for a directed verdict were made respectively by the parties. The plaintiff's motion was sustained."

Just a quotation from case: no indication that student understands any of this. Incorporating procedural step in facts step is all right in principle but it is poorly done here: no clear statement of procedural history (who won judgment in trial court?, who is appealing?)

Issue

a) The issue is whether the P failed to prove the existence of a K because there was no showing that the P accepted the offer of the D and communicated the acceptance of said offer; <u>or</u>

Wrong. Notice that this articulation of the issue from the case explicitly presents the D's formulation ("The contention of the defendant on appeal is ...").

b) As stated by the court: "the question...is whether the P established a prima facie case".

Wrong. Even though the court articulated the issue in this form, it is incorrect for you to use it. Its defects are: A) it inquiries soley about a legal conclusion (a <u>prima facie</u> case); B) it is too broad; (it does not focus on the exact legal question posed by the facts); and C) it fails to include any key facts from the instant fact situation. See preferable statement of issues on p. 28.

Wrong. A broad formulation of the issue leads to a broad formulation of the holding which could apply to many cases, not only this one. It also lacks any reference to instant key facts. Remember: a holding (and an issue) incorporates applicable rule and key facts to which it applies.

This sentence expresses a profound, underlying legal truth. A brief of a case, however, is not the place for such a statement, unless it illumines the holding (or issue, or statement of key facts).

What is significant is the legal reasoning which specifically explains and justifies the court's decision-making. In a brief, therefore, you concentrate on such reasoning. This exposition of the court's reasoning does not so concentrate. It also offends against another precept of case briefing: conciseness. Gradually you develop judgment in distinguishing this type of introductory exposition of basic rules from the

<u>Holding</u>

The holding is that P established a prima facie case and deserved the liquidated damages.

<u>Reasoning</u>

As the court stated, "the governing principle arises out of a fact situation...":

> It is almost a legal maxim "out of the facts the law arises, since, it there be no state of facts, there can be no question of law."

The court then discussed two conceptions of a K. The first conception is that a K is

> a promise, the performance of which the law recognizes as a duty and for a breach of which a remedy is given.

The second conception of Professor Williston:

> a promise which the promisor should reasonably expect to induce action or forbearance of a definite

legal reasoning which directly supports the holding.

> and substantial character on the part of the promisee, and which does induce such action or forbearance, is binding if injustice can be avoided only by enforcement of the promise.

In contrast to the above detail, an explanation of the difference between the two types of contracts is not specified. A clear understanding of this difference is essential to understand the case.

In addition, the court stressed that the law recognizes two kinds of contracts: a bilateral contract and, as here, a unilateral contract.

The first sentence is a masterpiece of confusion: A) it presupposes what was to be decided -- whether or not there was a contract; B) it mistakenly confuses the parties -- the D at trial was the appellant on this appeal. The P at trial was the appellee on this appeal. In this opinion, the court mostly used the trial labels: the seller was the P; the buyer was the D. Performance of the delivery of the machinery was the acceptance (which is not incidental) and the consideration. Professor Williston and *Corpus Juris* did *not* provide the necessary legal authority: they provided *persuasive authority*, not *binding authority*. The court's opinion set forth basic rules or principles, not policies.

There was a prima facie case here because the appellant performed the obligation imposed on him by the contract. The contract here was a unilateral contract and hence the performance by the appellant established the consideration (and incidentally the acceptance) which was necessary. Professor Williston, as a learned commentator, and especially his famous book on contracts, plus *Corpus Juris*, a well-known legal encyclopedia, provided the necessary authority for these basic legal policies.

There is no indication that the student knows that these prior precedents were binding on the court in the instant case.

In addition, there was other legal authority for this statement of law. See, e.g., *Hawkins v. Young*; and

> "Petroleum Products Distribution Co. v. Alton Tank Line, 165 Iowa, 398, 146

Do not include a string of citations.

N.W. 52; Rock Island Plow Co. v. Meredith, 107 Iowa, 498, 78 N.W. 233; McCormick Harveting Machines Co. v. Markert, 107 Iowa, 340, 78 N.W. 33. Pertinent language is used in McCormick Harvesting Machine Co., v. Richardson."

In McDermott v. Mahoney, the court, e.g., said:

Abbreviations would save valuable time.

"Where a written agreement signed by one party is accepted and adopted by the other, and acted upon, it becomes their contract in the same sense as though both parties had signed it."

This distinguishing was on the facts -- and that should be specified.

The court then distinguished a series of other cases from the instant case. These included:

Hargrove v. Crawford, 159 Iowa, 522, 141 N.W. 423; Durkee v. Schultz, 122 Iowa, 410, 98 N.W. 149; Doll & Smith v. A. & S. Sanitary Diary Co., 202 Iowa, 786, 211 N.W. 230.

Judgment for whom?

Judgment of trial court affirmed.

V. FUNCTION OF THE COURT EXEMPLIFIED IN PORT HURON

In McBoyle in Chapter II, the U.S. Supreme Court exemplified one of its functions: acting as the final judicial arbiter of a claim of error arising from a dispute over the meaning of a federal statute as applied to a particular fact situation. Here, in Port Huron, the function exemplified by the Supreme Court of Iowa is deciding a claim of error committed by the trial court arising from the application of a certain common law rule of contract to the instant fact situation. In contrast to McBoyle, where the claimed legal error arose from the trial court's application of a federal statute, the claim of error in Port Huron arises not from a rule based in a statute but rather from a rule rooted in case law. There is not a single reference in Port Huron to any statute. What the Iowa Supreme Court did in Port Huron is one function performed by appellate courts every day: deciding appeals which urge claims of legal error based on the application by a trial court of particular rules rooted in cases and resulting judge-made precedent.

Comment

I recognize that, as a beginner, studying and briefing Port Huron could easily take you a number of hours. Don't be discouraged: this is entirely normal in the beginning. In addition, don't be discouraged if you are confused and make mistakes: this too is entirely to be expected. Indeed, it is essential. You clarify your understanding of cases by gradually dispelling the swirling mist of confusion. In this quest for understanding of appellate cases, you are doing exercises in legal reasoning. Consciously and subconsciously, bit by bit, you are developing your basic skills in:

1) extricating key facts

2) issue-spotting and specification

3) selecting rules

4) applying rules to facts, especially by interweaving

5) adroitly using policy (not in Port Huron)

6) lawyerly writing

Relevance for Lawyering

As you struggle, it might encourage you if you clearly appreciate the relevance of what you are doing for actual lawyering. In practice, for example, a common question from a judge (at motion, trial or appellate levels) is -- "what does X case stand for?" If X case is Port Huron, cited in oral argument or written brief, your reply might be:

> Port Huron affirms the principle that for a unilateral contract the performance of the act requested in the offer is sufficient to establish acceptance.

This response is direct, precise and, therefore, lawyerly. To be able to boil down Port Huron in this way, your basic skills must be honed by briefing, classroom discussion, writing, etc. Remember the story of the French Impressionist painter who was challenged in a lawsuit over the fairness of a two-thousand-dollar price for a sketch he completed in two minutes. His reply: it required thirty-five years to learn how to do the sketch in two minutes. It may well take you hours to be able to boil Port Huron down to its legal essence. Take heart: what requires hours in the beginning will require a fraction of this time after your basic skills are sharpened.

The Principle of Port Huron

Some judges, and some first-year professors, will not ask "what does Port Huron stand for?" but rather will ask "what is the principle affirmed by Port Huron?" The response is the same as to the first question. In this identical response to the two questions, you have ommitted the specific illustration of "performance of the act requested in the offer," i.e., the plaintiff-seller's shipment of the farm machinery in Port Huron. That specific shipment is central to pinpointing the issue in controversy and the holding in Port Huron. Nevertheless, in responding to the hypothetical judge's question, or your professor's question, about the principle of Port Huron, you omit the fact of the shipment. What was critical to the formulation of the issue and holding in Port Huron is now omitted as a mere illustration. Why? The answer is that the judge and your professor are not asking about the issue and holding in Port Huron. Instead, their questions inquire about the principle which underlies this issue and holding. In understanding this principle, Port Huron becomes only an example of its application and the shipment of the farm machinery only one of many possible illustrations of it.

The Ratio Decidendi

Some first-year professors, but not judges, will also inquire of you about the ratio decidendi of a court's holding and judgment. That generally means a more general legal standard, either a principle or possibly a policy, which both underlies and compels the holding and judgment. Stated differently, it is that part of the court's reasoning absolutely required for its holding. Indeed, some first-year professors require you to include the ratio decidendi in the statement of the holding. In Port Huron, the ratio decidendi is clearly identical with the principle set forth above. In many cases, however, the ratio decidendi is not clear. Indeed, the waters are murky here in the use of ratio decidendi and the principle of a case. Don't expect scientific-type clarity. Do follow your professor's usage in each course.

Dicta

This culminating skill in catching the legal essence of a case also aids you in understanding the holding-dicta distinction. The holding here in response to the issue raised by the key facts is what the case has authoritatively decided. This is the law of the case. This is the precedent which triggers the application of stare decisis for future cases with similar facts and issues. This only is what the court has the power to decide, the particular issue in controversy which is before the court, and nothing else. When the holding is new, the court makes new law, judge-made law. When, as in Port Huron, the holding does not announce new law, it affirms an existing rule or principle of law.

In contrast, all reasoning which is not necessary for the holding is dicta. It may be undeniable, basic rules and maxims of law -- e.g., the introductory explanation in Port Huron that "out of the facts the law arises"; and the initial pedagogic review of basic contract rules. The point is not that dicta is necessarily unimportant. The point is that *dicta* in a case has a different legal status and consequence than the case holding. *Dicta* is not the law of the case and is not controlling for future cases with similar facts and issues.

Holdings

For many beginning students, learning the importance of case holdings leads to a typical first-year blunder: an obsession with holdings to the detriment of the key facts and the issues which led to the holdings and without which the holdings are *legally meaningless*. The utter fallacy inherent in this obsession should be apparent to you if you remember that the learning of legal reasoning is the *raison d'etre* of the first year.

VI. ISSUES NOT CONSIDERED AND DECIDED IN PORT HURON

Again, it may shed light to consider some of the many issues which were not considered and decided in *Port Huron* and to understand exactly why such issues were not considered and decided. These include the following:

Issues	Answers
A) Whether the defendant-buyer's claim that he cancelled his order (the offer necessary for a contract) was valid?	A) While this claim was advanced in the defendant's answer (a pre-trial pleading), the defendant at trial introduced "no evidence" at all. Ordinarily, an appellate court may not consider and decide an issue not considered and decided at trial. Ordinarily, an appellate court has no power to consider issues in the first instance ("de novo"), to receive evidence, and to decide them. Trial courts peform these tasks.
B) Whether the defendant had a good motive for trying (unsuccessfully) to cancel the contract?	B) Not a legal issue. Underlying motive is legally irrelevant here.
C) Whether the defendant's decision at trial to "introduce no evidence" was wise?	C) Not a legal issue for the trial or appellate court. Lawyers determine trial strategy and tactics.

D) Whether the price of $1,562.50 for the farm machinery was ethically justified?

D) Not a legal issue. Courts decide legal issues, not ethical issues.

E) Whether the price of $1,562.50 was economically justified?

E) Not a legal issue. Courts decide legal issues, not economic issues.

F) Whether the Supreme Court of Iowa should have referred this case back to the trial court with a recommendation that the plaintiff and defendant reach a negotiated settlement, or, failing that, they relitigate the facts and law.

F) Improper. Not the role of an appellate court. An appellate court (and a trial court) must decide the controversy presented to it by the parties (plaintiff and defendant). It may not decline to decide because it would prefer a negotiated settlement or because it regards judicial decision-making as unwise or difficult.

Moreover, an appellate court has <u>no power</u> to order a relitigation of the factual and legal issues decided at trial unless it finds legal error by the trial court which compels reversal or modification of the judgment of the trial court.

VII. <u>MORE DEFINITIONS</u>

1. A <u>Prima Facie Case</u> (at first view). Very simply, a <u>prima facie</u> case means that the plaintiff must introduce sufficient evidence at trial to establish the plaintiff's cause-of-action if it is assumed that such evidence is true and credible. Only then will the judge allow the case to go to the jury for fact-finding. Slightly elaborated, it means that the plaintiff at trial must introduce sufficient facts (e.g., testimony, documents, an "order for goods") which prove, if believed, each element of the legal claim asserted, so that the trial judge is satisfied that the jury could reasonably find a verdict for the plaintiff. The trial judge alone determines whether or not a <u>prima facie</u> case has been established. Sometimes, the <u>prima facie</u> case is called the <u>burden of production</u> (of producing evidence). In <u>Port Huron</u>, the plaintiff-seller introduced evidence (a written order and testimony) to prove that the plaintiff-seller and the defendant-buyer entered into a contract and that the defendant breached the contract, entitling the

plaintiff to money damages. The plaintiff's prima facie case consisted of evidence to prove the elements of a contract (offer, acceptance and consideration), breach of contract (refusal to accept delivery of the machinery), and damages (specified liquidated damages, freight charges, etc.).

2. Burden of Proof. Burden of proof has two meanings. The first meaning relates to the plaintiff's burden of proving a prima facie case.

Once the trial judge determines that a prima facie case has been established, the plaintiff, or prosecutor in a criminal case, then has a second challenge: to persuade the fact-finder (judge or jury) that all the evidence introduced at trial proves the legal claim asserted by the standard of a preponderance of the evidence (civil case) or by the standard of beyond a reasonable doubt (criminal case). This is the second and more usual meaning of burden of proof. It is also called the burden of persuasion. In Port Huron, a civil case, the breach of contract must be proved by a preponderance of the evidence.

The standard of a preponderance of the evidence in a civil case means that the totality of the credible evidence introduced (e.g., testimony, documents) outweighs, or is more convincing, than the evidence which is introduced against it.

The standard of beyond a reasonable doubt, the burden of proof on a prosecutor in a criminal case, means that the totality of the credible evidence introduced at trial (e.g., testimony, documents, physical evidence such as a gun) proves the defendant's guilt to a moral certainty, a level of proof which is convincing and which excludes reasonable theories of innocence. The standard of proof of beyond a reasonable doubt in a criminal case is more exacting than the standard of proof of a preponderance of the evidence in a civil case.

3. A Directed Verdict. In a directed verdict, the trial judge directs a verdict for one party against the other party. A motion for a directed verdict should be granted if all the evidence (the facts and inferences) "point so strongly and overwhelmingly in favor of one party that the Court [judge] believes that reasonable men could not arrive at a contrary verdict...." (Boeing Co. v. Shipman, 411 F.2d 365, 374 [5th Cir. 1969]). In considering whether or not to grant such a motion, a trial court must consider "all of the evidence..." from the standpoint "most favorable" to the party against whom the motion is made. In criminal cases, however, there can be no directed verdict against the defendant.

In Port Huron, the trial court granted the plaintiff-seller's motion for a directed verdict in its favor. The trial court apparently decided that since the defendant-buyer introducted "no evidence" at trial, there was no factual issue presented for the jury to decide. The only matter remaining was the application of a clear legal rule: for a unilateral contract, acceptance may be established by performance of the requested act. The trial court applied this rule to the undisputed facts and the result was clear. By granting the plaintiff's motion for a directed verdict, the trial court implicitly stated that no reasonable juror could find to the contrary. In rejecting the defendant-buyer's claim of legal error because of this directed verdict, the appellate court, the Supreme Court of Iowa, affirmed the legal correctness of the trial court's granting of the motion for a directed verdict for the plaintiff.

4. Complaint. In a common meaning in a civil case, a complaint is a formal written pleading by which a plaintiff initiates a legal proceeding against a defendant. A complaint asserts a legal claim, often called a cause-of-action, alleging a violation of a legal right of the plaintiff by the defendant. A complaint demands a remedy for this claimed violation. In Port Huron, the plaintiff-seller initiated a legal proceeding against the defendant-buyer with a complaint which alleged that the defendant-buyer breached his contractual duty owed to the plaintiff-seller by refusing to accept and pay for the farm machinery. For this claimed breach of contract, the plaintiff-seller demanded money damages as specified in the contract.

5. Answer. It has many different meanings as used in the cases. One of these meanings is a pre-trial pleading by a defendant in a civil case: an answer is a formal written response to the plaintiff's allegations in a complaint, setting forth the legal and factual allegations which comprise the basis of the defense. In Port Huron, this was the meaning of the court's use of the word: "(t)he defendant in his answer...but the allegation continued to rest in the answer." This word answer is an example of the use in opinions of words which have a common English meaning and a particular legal meaning (see p. 14).

6. Contract. A simple, much-quoted definition of a contract is set forth in the American Law Institute's Restatement of the Law of Contracts (sec.1).

> A contract is a promise or a set of promises for the breach of which the law gives a remedy, or the performance of which the law in some way recognizes as a duty.

7. Promisor. A promisor is simply a person who makes a promise.

8. Promisee. A promisee is simply a person to whom a promise is made.

9. Promise. A promise, like so many words used in cases, has multiple meanings. Its particular meaning must, therefore, be determined with each use. In the Restatement of the Law of Contracts by the American Law Institute (§2), a promise is defined as follows:

> ...a manifestation of intention to act or refrain from acting in a specified way, so made as to justify a promisee in understanding that a commitment has been made.

10. American Law Institute. An independent, private, law-reform organization composed of American judges, lawyers and professors which prepares model legislative codes in many areas of law for consideration by the various state legislatures. For example, its Model Penal Code has influenced many legislative recodificatins of state penal codes. Its Uniform Commercial Code has been adopted in many states. Its Restatements of Law (e.g., Torts, Contracts, Property) describe what the current state of law is in a particular area and specify changes that should take place, in the opinion of the American Law Institute.

I. INTRODUCTION

McBoyle is a case in criminal law which is an example of public law. It is the state against the defendant. In most first-year courses, however, it is not public law cases that you'll be studying. Rather, it is private law cases like Port Huron (civil, not criminal, cases) that you'll be scrutinizing in torts, contracts, property, civil procedure, etc. In these subjects, it is typically two individuals, a plaintiff and a defendant, who are the parties to the lawsuit. The state is not a party. The plaintiff, who initiates the lawsuit, claims that the defendant, by action or failure to act, has violated a legal right of the plaintiff, and hence, the plaintiff has suffered damages. For these damages, resulting from the defendant's violation, the plaintiff claims a remedy, usually money.

Using the six-step process and applying the guidelines detailed in Chapter II, please brief the following case in negligence (torts).

Neil Sauer, an Infant, by Ann Sauer, His Guardian ad Litem, et al., Respondents, *v.* Hebrew Institute of Long Island, Inc., Appellant.

First Department, November 27, 1962.

***

Appeal from a judgment of the Supreme Court, in favor of plaintiffs, entered April 6, 1962 in Bronx County, upon a decision of the court at a Trial Term (Charles A. Loreto, J.), without a jury.

Carl J. Silverstein of counsel (*Turetzky & Cohen,* attorneys), for appellant.

Joseph R. Apfel for respondents.

Bergan, J. The infant plaintiff, a camper at defendant's Summer camp, was injured while playing a game supervised by defendant's personnel. The infant was 13 years old and the game was a " water fight " between groups of campers of similar age, played on a grass-covered area in which opposing groups of boys doused each other with water from cups or water pistols.

In running away from an opponent, the infant plaintiff slipped on the grass and struck his head on a concrete walk at the side of the grass area. After a trial before the court without a jury, an award of $15,000 has been made to infant plaintiff and nominal damages to his father.

In our view of the record, this result is not warranted. The defendant, as the operator of a camp for boys, could not reasonably be made responsible in damages for the consequences of every possible hazard of play activity. It was required, rather, to guard against dangers which ought to have been foreseen in the exercise of reasonable care (*Klein* v. *Hoffman,* 15 A D 2d 899; *Weinstein* v. *Tunis Lake Props.,* 15 Misc 2d 432, affd. *sub nom. Derwin* v. *Tunis Lake Props.,* 9 A D 2d 960, motion for leave to appeal denied 10 A D 2d 711).

It has not been demonstrated that the water fight game was more hazardous than any ordinary camp activity involving running. It was inevitable in the game that the grass would become wet; and, indeed, in any such game among 13-year-old boys, that there would be tumbles and falls whether it was wet or dry.

To impose liability in this situation is to interdict the game itself, which in turn would so sterilize camping activity for boys as to render it sedentary. It would take a keen sense of the prescient to envisage that in running in the game the infant plaintiff would slip at the very point in the area where there was a concrete walk. Nor is it, indeed, clearly demonstrated that, in view of the infant plaintiff's bare feet, the wetness of the grass played any effective part in his falling.

The Trial Judge felt that the game itself " ha[d] every aspect of innocent play "; that the supervision was adequate and there was no " defect in the grounds on which the contest took place." (33 Misc 2d 785, 786.) He felt, however, that the game should have been played on sand and not on grass. This retrospective view of how the camp should have managed the game, upon which there can be reasonable difference of opinion, is insufficient to impose a liability on defendant, either as an evaluation of the facts of the case, or as a matter of law.

The judgment for plaintiffs should be reversed on the law and the facts and judgment entered for defendant, without costs.

Rabin, J. P., Valente, Eager and Steuer, JJ., concur.

Judgment for plaintiff unanimously reversed, on the law and on the facts, without costs and the complaint dismissed, without costs. Settle order on notice.

Contrast your brief of Sauer with the brief detailed below.

III. AN EXCELLENT BEGINNER'S BRIEF

Sauer v. Hebrew Instit.
17 App. Div.2nd 245
(1st Dept. 1962)

Comments

This statement of key facts emerges from application of guidelines set forth on pp. 23-5.

The appellate court used the trial court labels, the plaintiff and the defendant. The defendant was the appellant on appeal; the plaintiff was the respondent.

Facts

P, 13-year-old summer camper, participated in "water fight" between group of campers of similar age. "Water fight", supervised by employees of D-camp operator, played on grassy area; boys threw and shot water at each other. P ran, slipped on wet grass, "struck his head on concrete walk" next to grassy area and suffered injury.

These elements of the c/a of tort negligence are not set forth in the opinion. They are obtainable from other cases, casebook, hornbook, professor's lecture. You cannot understand this case without knowing the elements of this cause of action.

P initiated c/a for tort neg. Elements: 1) existence of duty; 2) reasonable person standard of care; 3) breach; 4) causation (factual and legal); and 5) actual damages. Conflict centered on elements (2) and (3).

Procedural History

Brief procedural history provides legal orientation: who won what at trial; who was appealing.

P awarded $15,000 f/neg. tort (father: nominal damages) after trial without jury. D-camp operator appeals.

Issue

One-sentence, issue-specificacation in question form. It incorporates some key facts, refers to applicable rule and pinpoints elements of rule at issue.

Is the D-camp operator liable in negligent tort for breaching its duty "to guard against dangers" which "ought to have been foreseen" in exercising reasonable care when a 13-year-old camper runs, slips and hurts his head on concrete during a supervised "water fight"?

Holding

Statement of holding: an answer to issue, incorporating some key facts meshed together with reference to applicable rule and pinpointing of elements of rule at issue. This is the law of the case.

No. The D-camp operator is not liable in negligent tort for breaching its duty to guard against dangers it ought to have foreseen in exercising reasonable care when a 13-year-old camper runs, falls and is hurt on concrete while participating in a supervised "water fight."

Judgment

Judgment is the result or disposition of the case.

Judgment of trial court for P reversed by appellate court.

Reasoning

This presentation of the court's reasoning identifies and categorizes the two major types of argument. By so doing, this presentation reflects apparent student understanding of the court's reasoning. The first argument concentrated on tying together key facts in an argument that the water fight was "innocent play" without fault by the D.

First, factually, the ct. stressed that "tumbles and falls" are inevitable in "ordinary camp activity"; that there was no evidence that the water fight was riskier than any "activity involving running"; that the trial judge found that the water fight was "innocent play" with adequate supervision and no defect in grassy site of game. Trial judge's view that sandy area would have provided better game site was merely one retrospective opinion.

The policy argument concentrated on the desirable purposes served by the court's holding. Summer camp activity for boys can have a certain roughness. A contrary holding might bar such games and make such camping "sedentary."

Second, the ct. stressed the policy implications of finding liability on these facts: it would "interdict the game itself" and "sterilize camping activity for boys" making it "sedentary." Who could foresee that the P would fall on this concrete walk? In essence, the ct. said that tort negligence does not -- and should not -- impose liability for harms from "every possible hazard of play activity" -- only for those D ought to have foreseen in exercising reasonable care.

Do you understand how the two arguments together provided an explanation and justification for the holding?

Comment

With the focus that comes from experience and confidence, at least the reasoning could be set forth more succinctly. For example:

Reasoning

1) Factual Argum.

"tumbles and falls" inevitable in "innocent play"

no E of greater risk than in any camp running game

no Mon. am. quarterbacking on site selection by tr. judge

2) Policy Argum.

Finding D liable here would:

"interdict" water fights

"sterilize camp act. f/ boys." Risk here not foreseeable in exercising reas. care

IV. A POOR BRIEF

Comments

Cryptic. Omissions include:

A) supervision
B) concrete at the side of wet grassy area where game occurred
C) campers of similar age
D) P was running
E) elements of c/a for tort negligence
F) elements of c/a apparently at issue

The procedural history step of the brief is omitted.

Facts

A young boy fell on concrete and hurt his head while engaged in a "water fight" with other summer campers. He received damages.

Issue

Far too broad a specification of issue. This is not the issue posed by these facts. This statement is a conclusory legal formulation which totally ignores the key facts.

Is it reasonable to make the camp operator liable in tort negligence "for the consequences of every possible hazard of play activity"?

Holding

An incorrect, broad issue-specification leads to an incorrect, broad statement of the holding. It provides <u>no</u> guidance to correct legal standard to be applied in deciding when liablity should exist for which hazards.

No. A camp operator is not liable in tort negligence "for the consequences of every possible hazard of play activity."

The court's judgment, meaning the result or disposition, is omitted.

Reasoning

Not a reason. Rather, it is part of the correct holding (see p. 85).

The ct. stated that a camp operator is only required "to guard against dangers which ought to have been foreseen in the exercise of reasonable care. (<u>Klein v. Hoffman</u>, 15 A D 2d 899; <u>Weinstein v. Tunis Lake Props.</u>, 15 Misc. 2d 432, affd. <u>sub</u>. <u>nom</u>. <u>Derwin v. Tunis Lake Props.</u>, 9 A D 2d 960, motion for leave to appeal denied 10 A D 2d 711)."

Unnecessary to include string of citations.

The ct. also stressed the following:

This represents an effort to identify steps in the court's reasoning. It is also necessary, however, to categorize types of argument (e.g. factual, policy, persuasive authority) in order to understand the reasoning. Not all arguments are of equal legal

A) no demonstration that water fight was "more hazardous than any ordinary camp activity involving running"

B) inevitable that in game "grass would become wet" and that "13-year-old boys" will tumble and fall "whether" grass "was wet or dry" status or of equal importance in a particular case.

C) "To impose liability in this situation is to interdict the game itself, which in turn would so sterilize camping activity for boys as to render it sedentary. It would take a keen sense of the prescient to envisage that in running in the game the infant plaintiff would slip at the very point in the area where there was a concrete walk."

D) the trial judge said the game was "innocent play"; that the supervision was adequate and there was no "defect" in the grounds on which the contest took place

Extensive quotation is no substitute for identifying and understanding the particular types of argument.

E) he felt, however, "that the game should have been played on sand and not on grass. This retrospective view of how the camp should have managed the game, upon which there can be reasonable difference of opinion, is insufficient to impose a liability on defendant, either as an evaluation of the facts of the case, or as a matter of law."

V. <u>COMMENT</u>

Perhaps you have noticed that the element most at issue here -- a requirement "to guard against dangers which ought to have been foreseen in the exercise of reasonable care" -- is quite abstract. You might ask yourself: which dangers ought to be foreseeable and what does reasonable care mean? Your initial reaction that various judges might easily decide differently the meaning of this element of the rule as applied to particular fact situations is borne out by the case that follows below.

You do know something, however, from this <u>Sauer</u> case. You know that the holding not only disposes of this case: it is also a precedent which must be applied by this court in future cases with <u>similar</u> facts and issues. That is a requirement of <u>stare decisis</u> which is central to our common law system. The holding is binding authority for this appellate court and for all inferior (subordinate) courts for future cases with similar facts and issues.

With this in mind, please brief the following case, also in the same appellate court as decided Sauer. Apply the steps and guidelines set forth in Chapter II. Your professor has asked you to "reconcile" these two cases -- i.e., to explain the facts, issues, holdings and reasoning, as consistent (if you believe them to be so) or inconsistent (if you so believe). One hint: concentrate on exactly how the facts in the two cases are the same and exactly how they are different.

RICHARD GREAVES, an Infant, by His Mother and Natural Guardian, ADRIENNE GREAVES, et al., Respondents, v BRONX Y.M.C.A., Appellant.

First Department, June 24, 1982

SUMMARY

APPEAL from a judgment of the Supreme Court in favor of plaintiffs, entered December 12, 1980, in Bronx County, upon a verdict rendered at a Trial Term (ALFRED J. CALLAHAN, J.).

***

APPEARANCES OF COUNSEL

Harvey J. Lippman of counsel (*Norman S. Goldsmith* and *Shari B. Rubin* with him on the brief; *Jones, Hirsch & Bull,* attorneys), for appellant.

Philip Hoffer of counsel (*Rose Hoffer, Frank J. Giordano* and *Harold Weisman* with him on the brief; *Frank J. Giordano, P.C.,* attorney), for respondents.

OPINION OF THE COURT

SANDLER, J.

Defendant appeals from a judgment for the infant plaintiff after a jury trial in an action for damages sustained when the plaintiff, then nine years old, was a camper at defendant's camp.

***

From the evidence presented by the plaintiff, the jury could reasonably have concluded that he sustained a severe injury to his elbow when he fell during the course of a game of ring-a-levio; that both campers and counselors participated in the game, the counselors as a separate team of "catchers"; that the game was played on a sloping grass area adjacent to a swimming pool; that the plaintiff slipped on a section of the grass that was damp as a result of water spilling over from the pool and the counselors having previously hosed the campers when they had emerged from the pool.

The principal issue presented on this appeal is the legal sufficiency of the evidence, the defendant contending that the case is controlled by the decision in *Sauer v Hebrew Inst. of Long Is.* (17 AD2d 245, affd 13 NY2d 913) in which, in a similar factual situation, a verdict in favor of the plaintiff was reversed, on the law and on the facts, and the complaint was dismissed.

As described in this court's decision in *Sauer (supra)*, the plaintiff in that case, then 13 years old, was injured at a summer camp while playing a game supervised by the defendant's personnel. The game was a "water fight" between groups of campers of similar age, played on a grass-covered area in which opposing groups of boys doused each other with water from cups or water pistols. Running away from an opponent, the plaintiff in *Sauer* slipped on the grass and struck his head on a concrete walk on the side of the grass area.

In reversing a verdict after a nonjury trial in favor of the plaintiff, the court said (at p 246): "The defendant, as the operator of a camp for boys, could not reasonably be made responsible in damages for the consequences of every possible hazard of play activity. It was required, rather, to guard against dangers which ought to have been foreseen in the exercise of reasonable care".

Further on in the opinion, the following was said (p 246): "To impose liability in this situation is to interdict the game itself, which in turn would so sterilize camping activity for boys as to render it sedentary."

Recognizing the similarity of this case to the situation in *Sauer (supra)*, we are not persuaded that *Sauer* is dispositive. The effect here of finding the evidence legally sufficient to support the jury's verdict would not be "to interdict the game itself". At issue here is not the appropriateness of the game that was played for the youngsters involved, but rather the judgment of the supervising counselors in selecting for the playing of the game a surface that might reasonably have been foreseen as adding needlessly to the risks inherent in the game itself.

It is appreciated that difficult problems of judgment may often confront counselors supervising the play activity of youngsters accustomed to strenuous physical exertions often accompanied by actions that involve some degree of risk. We appreciate the concern that a finding of liability in some camp situations may tend to "sterilize camping [activities] for boys as to render it sedentary." On the facts which the jury might reasonably have found in this case, however, we believe that a factual issue for jury determination was presented as to whether the playing of the game here on the described surface involved a foreseeable risk of unjustifiable danger. (See *Quinlan v Cecchini,* 41 NY2d 686, 689.)

Accordingly, the judgment of the Supreme Court, Bronx County (CALLAHAN, J.), entered on December 12, 1980, after a jury trial in favor of plaintiff for $90,000 should be affirmed.

Again, contrast your brief of <u>Greaves</u> with the following brief.

VII. AN EXCELLENT BEGINNER'S BRIEF

Greaves v. Bronx Y.M.C.A.
87 App. Div. 2d 394 (1st Dept. 1982)

Comments

This is a direct, fairly succinct statement of key facts. Again, the appellate court used the trial court labels, the plaintiff and the defendant. The defendant at trial was the appellant on appeal; the plaintiff at trial was the appellee on appeal.

Facts

P, 9-year-old summer camper, fell during a game of "ring-a-levio," and severely injured his elbow. Campers and counselors participated as separate teams. Game played "on a sloping grass area adjacent to a swimming pool." Grass wet. P initiated c/a f/tort neg. Elements: same as in <u>Sauer</u>, see p. 84. Again, conflict centers on elements 2) and 3), see p. 84.

Brief, accurate statement of what happened at trial and who was appealing.

Procedural History

P won judgment for $90,000 for neg. tort after trial. D-camp operator appeals.

This formulation of the issue in question form incorporates key facts, reference to applicable rule, and pinpointing of elements of the rule at issue.

Issue

Whether the D-camp operator is liable in negligent tort for counselors' failing to foresee in exercising reasonable care that the selection of a sloping, wet, grassy area adjacent to a pool on which the P fell and was injured while playing "ring-a-levio" "added needlessly to the risks inherent in the game itself"?

This is concrete statement of the law of the case: a reference to the general rule and elements of the

Holding

Yes. The D-camp operator is liable in negligent tort for counselors' failing to foresee in exercising reasonable care rule, applied to particular facts of case.

The trial court judgment for plaintiff is affirmed.

The holding in Sauer is a controlling precedent for this case unless the court finds the instant facts to be distinguishable. It is imperative, therefore, to scrutinize exactly how facts are similar and exactly how they are different.

Since fact patterns in different cases will always be different in some ways, the real question is which differences are sufficient to render the facts not similar and hence distinguishable. No exact formula, no calculas, exists for this legal determination. In essence, it is a matter of lawyerly experience, judgment and argument. While both game sites were wet and grassy, the site selected here was sloping and next to a pool. Using these facts to distinguish the facts in Sauer is an exercise in judgment and argument, not an ex cathedra pronouncement from Zeus on Mount Olympus.

that the selection of a sloping, wet, grassy area adjacent to a pool on which the P ran, fell and was injured while playing "ring-a-levio", "added needlessly to the risks inherent in the game itself."

Judgment

Judg. f/P f/$90,000 affirmed.

Reasoning

1) The ct. concentrates on distinguishing the facts of this case from the facts in Sauer. As related by the ct., the facts are similar in many ways:

Sauer	Greaves
summer camp	summer camp
water fight	ring-a-levio
grassy area	grassy area
P fell and was injured	P fell and was injured

The related facts are also different in some ways.

Sauer	Greaves
13-year-old P	9-year-old P
counselors supervised game	counselors played in game
P fell on concrete	P fell on grass
no defect in wet grassy site of game	wet grassy site of game was sloping and next to pool.

Of all these differences, the ct. weighted the particular fact that the supervising counselors selected this sloping, wet, grassy area next to the pool as presenting a question for the jury: did this selection add needlessly to the inherent risks of the game?

Ct. concluded that Sauer is not "dispositive," meaning that the holding in Sauer was not controlling here in Greaves. Why? Facts presented in Greaves were distinguishable from Sauer. Hence, the Sauer precedent was not applicable.

Court agreed with the policy purposes presented in Sauer and argued that its holding here was fully consistent with such policy purposes.

2) In an analysis of the policy purposes presented in Sauer, the ct. agreed that such games should not be "interdict[ed]" so as to "sterilize camping" activities and render them "sedentary." Ct. argued, however, that it was not doing this but only evaluating the judgment of the counselors in selecting a dangerous site for the game to be played.

Comment

If you happen to find the court's basis for distinguishing the facts in Sauer from the facts here in Greaves less than fully persuasive, you are in good company. A dissenter in the appellate court case, Justice Bloom, joined by Presiding Justice Murphy, also disagreed.

Please brief this dissent. In briefing a dissent, you should ordinarily be more succinct than in briefing the court's opinion. You should analyze a dissent to determine exactly how its marshalling of the facts, its formulation of the issue, its proposed holding and its reasoning contrast with comparable elements in the court's opinion, i.e., the opinion of the majority.

Bloom, J. (dissenting). In August, 1976, plaintiff, then nine years of age, was enrolled in a summer day camp operated by defendant. On the day in question, plaintiff, and the others participating in the day camp, were at the Castle Hill Beach Club. In the late afternoon the campers emerged from the club pool. Their evening activity was to go to a Yankee baseball game. As they exited from the pool they were hosed down in accordance with the usual custom. They then dressed and had a typical camp supper consisting of hot dogs and hamburgers grilled at a barbecue pit. Since there was time to spare before they proceeded to the Yankee Stadium the campers and counselors engaged in a game of "ring-a-levio". The team of chasers consisted of three or four counselors while the team of those chased consisted of campers.

As the chase proceeded, plaintiff, who was dressed in jeans, a shirt, socks and sneakers, fell and injured his arm. He was taken to a hospital where it was ascertained that his elbow was broken. The arm was placed in a cast and plaintiff remained in the hospital for five days. Within three months the arm had healed and since that time plaintiff has actively engaged in athletics.

Thereafter this action was brought. It is bottomed on the claim that the "ring-a-levio" chase took place in an area surrounding the pool and that the defendant was negligent in permitting the game to be played in the vicinity of the pool. Plaintiff's fall, it is contended, resulted from the chase, during which he slipped on wet or damp grass. The jury returned a verdict in favor of the plaintiff in the sum of $250,000, and allocated 60% of the negligence to defendant and 40% to the infant plaintiff.

***

We are of the opinion that this case is governed by our holding in *Sauer v Hebrew Inst. of Long Is.* (17 AD2d 245, affd 13 NY2d 913). Accordingly, we would reverse and dismiss the complaint. In *Sauer* the plaintiff was a camper at defendant's summer camp. The campers were engaged in a game of "waterfight" in which the contending teams sought to douse their adversaries with water from cups or water pistols. Plaintiff, in an endeavor to avoid being sprayed with water, ran from an opponent. In so doing he slipped on the wet grass and struck his head on a concrete area immediately adjacent to the wet grassy area on which he slipped. In exonerating the defendant from liability we noted (p 246):

"The defendant, as the operator of a camp for boys, could not reasonably be made responsible in damages for the consequences of every possible hazard of play activity. It was required, rather, to guard against dangers which ought to have been foreseen in the exercise of reasonable care * * *

"It has not been demonstrated that the water fight game was more hazardous than any ordinary camp activity involving running. It was inevitable in the game that the grass would become wet; and, indeed, in any such game among 13-year-old boys, that there would be tumbles and falls whether it was wet or dry.

"To impose liability in this situation is to interdict the game itself, which in turn would so sterilize camp activity for boys as to render it sedentary".

***

The falls and tumbles of a nine year old at play are an inherent risk of any physical, competitive game. Only by forbidding the game can the risk be guarded against. However, to interdict such games is to make children's camping activities little more than a "baby-sitting" operation. Much as the law devotes itself to the protection of children it is powerless to protect them against childhood itself.

FEIN and ASCH, JJ., concur in the opinion of SANDLER, J.;

***

MURPHY, P. J., and BLOOM, J., dissent in an opinion by BLOOM, J.

Judgment, Supreme Court, Bronx County, entered on December 12, 1980, affirmed.

IX. AN EXCELLENT BEGINNER'S BRIEF OF THE DISSENT

Comments

What the dissent illustrates is that legal reasoning is not mechanistic. Marshalling facts and arguments isn't simply identifying and categorizing them: it's also weighting them -- i.e., deciding which facts and arguments deserve to have more importance than others.

The dissenters obviously believed that the key facts were that the P participated in a rough-house game of "ring-a-levio" in which, as in any running game, "falls and tumbles" were inevitable. The fact of the sloping, wet, grassy site of the game was not weighted as important and it was not seen as the source of harm.

Note the power of this simple sentence. It is outstanding legal writing.

Brief

Factually, the dissent did not single out the counselors' judgment in selecting the sloping, wet, grassy area next to the pool as presenting added, foreseeable dangers to those inherent in playing game. Instead, it referred, in cursory and mostly conclusory language, to P's claim that the "ring-a-levio" chase took place "in an area surrounding the pool and that D was negligent in permitting the game to be played in the vicinity of the pool" where P slipped on wet grass.

The dissenters clearly believed that the harm to P came from the dangers inherent in the game itself, not from the selected site. Such a fall as P suffered is "an inherent" risk of any physical, competitive running game. Only by forbidding the game can the risk be guarded against. In an eloquent sentence, the dissenters summed up their view:

> Much as the law devotes itself to the protection of children it is powerless to protect them againt childhood itself.

The dissenters did not, therefore, find facts of <u>Sauer</u> distinguishable. Thus, the holding of <u>Sauer</u> was controlling. The D-camper operator on these facts did not breach its duty "to guard against dangers which ought to have been foreseen in the exercise of reasonable care."

X. FUNCTIONS OF THE COURT EXEMPLIFIED IN SAUER AND IN GREAVES

Reviewing Application of Judge-Made Rules At Trial

1) In Port Huron in Chapter III, the Supreme Court of Iowa decided a claim of error committed by the trial court arising from the application at trial of a certain judge-made rule of contract to that fact situation. Here, in Sauer and in Greaves, the Appellate Division (First Department) of the New York State Supreme Court (which is the intermediate appellate court in New York State) decided a claim of legal error committed by the trial court arising from the application at trial of a certain judge-made rule of tort negligence to the fact situations embodied in Sauer and in Greaves. As in Port Huron, there is not a single reference in Sauer and in Greaves to any statute. This reflects the common-law truth that rules of tort negligence are substantially rooted in cases and in resulting case law. Court decisions in tort negligence cases usually flow from analysis of prior tort cases, not from analysis of statutes.

2) More specifically, in Sauer, the Appellate Division (First Department) decided that the trial judge in Sauer committed legal error in deciding in favor of the plaintiff. Why? As stated previously, the facts introduced as evidence by the plaintiff did not establish a breach of the defendant's duty to guard against dangers it ought to have foreseen in the exercise of reasonable care. Stated differently, the plaintiff did not meet its burden of proof (see p. 78) on these elements of reasonable care and breach.

In Greaves, however, the appellate court rejected the defendant's claim of legal error, deciding that the facts therein were sufficient to spell out a breach of the defendant's duty to guard against dangers it reasonably ought to have foreseen. Implicitly, the court here was affirming that the plaintiff at trial did meet his burden of proof on these elements of reasonable care and breach.

Fact-Finding

3) In making these decisions, the appellate court was not deciding what are called questions of fact: e.g., it was not deciding that the plaintiff's witnesses were more credible (believable) than the defendant's witnesses; it was not determining the extent of the plaintiff's injury. All of that was decided by the fact-finder at trial. In Sauer, the trial judge acted as fact-finder because the case was tried without a jury. In Greaves, the jury acted as fact-finder (the traditional role of the jury). The appellate court did not -- and had no power to -- substitute its finding of facts for that of the fact-finder. Instead, its review was of claims of legal error committed by the trial judge -- i.e., the facts, as found by the fact-finder at trial, did not establish a prima facie case. As a beginner, the appellate court review of this claim of legal error may appear to you to present a factual question. It does not. The categorizing of issues as either legal or factual is itself a matter of legal determination. To avoid confusion, follow your professor's guidance and observe how judges categorize issues in opinions.

Stare Decisis

4) In deciding Greaves, the appellate court is exemplifying its role in adhering to the fundamental doctrine of stare decisis. In its opinion, stare decisis is not explicitly discussed. It is presupposed. It underlies the dissenters' contention (see court's opinion, p. 91) that "the case is controlled by the decision in Sauer" and the dissenters' statement (see p. 96) that "[w]e are of the opinion that this case is governed by our holding in Sauer." Stare decisis is the trigger for the struggle over the facts: are they sufficiently similar to the facts in Sauer? If so, there is ordinarily no escape: the precedent in Sauer must apply. If they are distinguishable, the precedent of Sauer is not controlling.

Just as judges argue that a second case is controlled, or not controlled, by a prior case, you will argue in class that two or more cases are consistent or not consistent. This is called reconciling and synthesizing cases. Typically, you will be queried (cross-examined may be more accurate) on exactly how the facts in two or more cases are the same and different. In addition, you may then be asked about the legal significance of these similarities and differences. Do the similarities explain the court's similar or different formulation of the issue, its specification of the holding and its reasoning? After scrutinizing the judges' reasoning in Greaves, it should be clear to you how fundamental is the process of reconciling and synthesizing cases.

No Ad-Hoc Decision-Making

5) There is an underlying principle animating the courts in both Sauer and Greaves. Neither trial nor appellate courts may engage in ad-hoc decision-making, seeking to do the "right thing" in each case in disregard of applicable rules and principles. Instead, courts must decide the particular controversy presented to it by the fact situation only in light of a more general rule or principle which covers a group of like controversies. Ad-hoc decision-making is rejected in our system of law.

XI. ISSUES NOT CONSIDERED AND DECIDED IN SAUER AND GREAVES

Once again, it may be clarifying to enumerate some of the many issues not considered and decided in Sauer and Greaves and to understand exactly why such issues were not considered and decided. These include the following:

Issues	Answers
A) Whether "water fights" and "ring-a-levio" were played in the past without mishap?	Irrelevant to the issue of breach of duty on specific occasions at issue.

B) Whether the rules of these games were fair?	Irrelevant. Courts are not arbiters of the fairness of games.
C) Whether the trial judges and jurors had played these games and therefore were competent to decide?	Irrelevant. Their authority to decide comes not from their experience at the games but from their status as judges and jurors.
D) Whether the campers could have played safer games than a "water fight" and "ring-a-levio"?	Irrelevant. Courts do not engage in such speculation -- such "what might have been."
E) Whether general court rules should be pronounced guiding camp operators in conducting games in the future?	A court decides only the particular controversy presented to it. It does not usually engage in such precautionary guideline formulations, however useful it might be to do so. (Perhaps, such guidelines are an issue for an executive licensing agency.)
F) Whether the trial judge thoroughly investigated all the facts involved in these injuries.	Wrong. A judge in our system of law is <u>not</u> an investigator. A court ordinarily decides <u>only</u> the facts and issues presented to it by the parties.
G) Whether these nonprofit, charitable defendants have funds to pay a judgment for damages?	Irrelevant to the determination of liability and damages.
H) Whether the trial judges are liberal or conservative in their views on tort negligence?	Irrelevant. Their sworn duty is to select and apply the applicable rules, not their personal views.
I) Whether these defendant-camp operators could claim a defense of freedom of religion?	Irrelevant. The issue is not an exercise of religious freedom but rather whether or not their conduct complied with their tort duty.
J) Whether the issue, holding and reasoning should apply to a summer camp for girls.	Irrelevant. A court decides <u>only</u> the controversy presented to it.
K) Whether these are sexist assumptions underlying the courts' discussions in <u>Sauer</u>	Perhaps, but what is the legal significance of that insight on the rights and duties of the

and Greaves of appropriate summer camp activities for boys?	plaintiffs and defendants in Sauer and Greaves? The insight may be true but irrelevant in both Sauer and Greaves.

XII. COMMENT

Sauer and Greaves provide an opportunity for understanding the role of a lawyer, not as an advocate for a party in a lawsuit, but rather as a counselor. Suppose you represented a camp operator, "Happy Times Camp" in 1962. Your client, the owner, had heard of the Sauer case from friends who operated the camp in Sauer. Your client asked you -- "does Sauer mean I can tell the counselors to relax -- they don't have to worry about the sites they select for water fights and other games?" In your lawyerly role as counselor, you might well have urged the camp operator to continue to direct the counselors to exercise not reasonable care but all possible care, both in selecting sites and in supervising games. In giving such advice, your objective is not simply to win a future lawsuit but to prevent injuries and lawsuits. Your client's interests, and the campers' interests, are best served if injuries and lawsuits are prevented. Such advice which exceeds your client's legal obligation serves moral and social interests which are promoted by the law. In addition, if your client later heard of the Greaves result in 1982, he would be especially delighted that he had followed your advice. The role of a lawyer as counselor can be an honorable and socially constructive role.

XIII. ADDITIONAL DEFINITIONS

1. Torts (tortious conduct). The American Law Institute's Restatement of the Law of Torts (Second) defines tortious conduct broadly as:

> ...conduct whether of act or omission... of such a character as to subject the actor to liability under the principles of the law of torts.

Major categories of such tort liability are specified:

A) "an act which is intended to cause an invasion of an interest legally protected against intentional invasion," meaning intentional torts such as assault and battery (A slaps B in the face), false imprisonment, trespass, conversion, libel and slander; or

B) "conduct which is negligent as creating an unreasonable risk of invasion of a legally protected interest, meaning negligent tort illustrated in Sauer and Greaves; and

C) "conduct which is carried on at the risk that the actor shall be subject to liability for harm caused thereby, although no such harm is intended and the harm cannot be prevented by any precautions or care which it is practicable to require," meaning strict liability tort -- e.g., liability for harm resulting from an unforeseeable defect in the brakes of a car.

2. Duty. The Restatement of the Law of Torts (Second) defines duty as denoting:

> the fact that the actor is required to conduct himself in a particular manner at the risk that if he does not do so he becomes subject to liabiliy to another to whom the duty is owed for any injury sustained by such other, of which that actor's conduct is a legal cause.

In Sauer and Greaves, the plaintiffs contended that the defendant-camp operators breached a duty owed to the plaintiffs. This particular duty in conducting games is to guard against dangers which ought to be foreseeable in the exercise of reasonable care, a duty grounded in tort negligence. In Sauer, the appellate court held that no such breach occurred. In Greaves, the same appellate court held that such a breach did occur.

3. Liability. While there are many possible meanings which must be particularized in each case, one simple definition is to be "bound or obligated in law...responsible; answerable." Somewhat elaborated, it means that a person (or entity) is legally responsible to another person (or entity) to account for a breach of duty, either by action or failure to act, which has caused a harm to such other person (or entity), and for which breach and harm the law gives a remedy (e.g., money damages). In both Sauer and Greaves, the trial courts imposed liability on the defendant-camp operators--viz, judgments for plaintiffs for money damages. In Sauer, that imposition of liability was reversed by the appellate court; in Greaves it was upheld. In Port Huron in Chapter III, the judgment at trial for the plaintiff-seller for money damages imposed liability on the defendant-buyer and was affirmed by the appellate court. In McBoyle in Chapter II, the judgment of conviction at trial imposed criminal liability for the federal crime of interstate transportation of a stolen vehicle knowing it to be stolen, but the judgment of conviction was overturned by the Supreme Court.

4. Infant and Guardian Ad Litem. An infant is a person who has not yet reached the age of legal capacity or competence, sometimes

called legal majority. At common law, twenty-one years was the dividing line; today, in most states, it is eighteen years. Please recognize, however, that this general rule has many particular exceptions from state to state. For example, driving licenses may be obtained at a younger age. Drinking alcoholic beverages in bars may not be legal until nineteen or twenty or twenty-one. In determining responsibility for crimes, the age varies; often it is sixteen but for some serious crimes (e.g., murder), sometimes younger.

In Sauer and Greaves, the plaintiffs were infants because they were nine and thirteen years old. They therefore lacked the legal capacity to initiate a lawsuit. Such a lawsuit is, therefore, typically initiated by a parent (or substitute) who is appointed a guardian ad litem. As stated by one court:

> A guardian ad litem is a special guardian appointed by the court to prosecute or defend, in behalf of an infant, a suit to which he is a party....Such a guardian is considered an officer of the court to represent the interests of the infant in the litigation.

XIV. A POSTSCRIPT: NARROW VERSUS BROAD STATEMENTS OF HOLDING AND PRECEDENT

What you have learned so far are the basics of briefing and using cases for legal reasoning. In this postscript, I highlight a somewhat more advanced technique: narrower versus broader statements of a holding and the resulting precedent. The following four examples begin with a quite narrow statement of the Greaves holding and progressively broaden the statement of the Greaves holding by more general language. You'll recall the following statement of the holding in the excellent brief of Greaves:

> The D-camp operator is liable in negligent tort for counselors' failing to foresee in exercising reasonable care that the selection of a sloping, wet, grassy area adjacent to a pool on which P ran, fell and was injured while playing "ring-a-levio," "added needlessly to the risks inherent" in the game itself.

Please contrast this statement with the following, alternative statement of the holding in Greaves:

> The D-camp operator is liable in negligent tort for counselors' failing to foresee in exercising reasonable care that the selection of a site for the playing of a running game on which the P

> ran, fell and was injured, "added needlessly to the risks inherent" in the game itself.

Notice that the second statement of the holding is somewhat more general. Instead of the specific words "selection of a sloping, wet, grassy area adjacent to a pool," the latter statement refers more generally to "selection of a site." Instead of the specific words "playing ring-a-levio," the latter statement refers more generally to "playing of a running game." The effect of the more general language is to broaden the holding somewhat and hence to enlarge the scope of future cases to which this precedent clearly applies. For example, selection of a site with holes or selection of a site near a cliff or selection of a site for the playing of tag would manifestly be covered by the general language. This somewhat broader statement of the holding is also a perfectly proper specification of the Greaves holding. The prior statement of the holding is not wrong. It is simply a narrower or stricter statement (though some of your professors may regard it as too narrow).

Contrast the previous two statements of the holding with the following, alternative statement of the holding in Greaves. Concentrate on exactly how it is the same and exactly how it is different.

> The D-camp operator is liable in negligent tort for injuries caused by supervisors' failing to foresee in exercising reasonable care that its supervisory efforts "added needlessly to the risks inherent" in camp activities.

Notice that this statement of the Greaves holding is substantially more abstract. Instead of "selection of a site" and "playing of a running game," you have the more general words "its supervisory efforts...." Instead of the words, "the P ran, fell and was injured," you have the more general words, "injuries caused by supervisors' failing...." While this statement of the Greaves holding is quite broad, your interest in arguing for the broader holding as the Greaves precedent would be appropriate if you represent a camper who was injuried by lightning when the camp hiking director told the campers to take shelter under a lone tree during a lightning storm. A hike is not a game but it is surely "a camp activity" and the "supervisory efforts" of the hiking director clearly "added needlessly to the risks inherent" in a camp activity during a lightning storm.

Naturally, your adversary, the lawyer for the camp operator, would argue that this statement of the Greaves holding and precedent is erroneous because it is too broad: it goes far beyond the facts of Greaves. The Greaves holding and precedent, your adversary would argue, should be limited to the facts of Greaves and similar facts, i.e., selection of a site for a running game, not selection of a site for shelter during a lightning storm. You would respond: a) that these differences in facts do not distinguish the two cases because the facts are similar and it is not required that the facts be identical for Greaves to be controlling;

and b) that this broader view of Greaves embodies its principle, what is sometimes called its ratio decidendi (see p. 75).

Who is correct? The trial judge who has to decide the new case provides the answer. The law authorizes a judicial decision-making procedure which results in a judgment for the plaintiff or for the defendant in the new case. If the issue is reviewed on appeal, the appellate judges will also decide by affirming or reversing the judgment of the trial court.

Lawyers and commentators (legal analysts) may disagree in law reviews or other articles or at meetings of bar association committees; they may even clearly have the more insightful analyses. Nevertheless, the decision of the court remains (until reversed or overruled). Why? The judges, not the lawyers and commentators, have the power to decide cases. The question is not which argument is correct in a philosophical, scientific or "objective" sense, but rather, which argument will be accepted and applied by a judge in a new case.

Consider, finally, this fourth statement of the Greaves holding and precedent:

> The D-camp operator is liable in negligent tort for injuries caused by its failing to foresee in exercising reasonable care that its actions "added needlessly to the risks inherent" in camp activities.

This is by far the broadest statement of the Greaves holding and precedent. Indeed, it is vulnerable precisely because it is too abstract, too sweeping, and so far removed from the key facts of Greaves: the counselors' selection of a sloping, wet, grassy site adjacent to a pool for the playing of "ring-a-levio" and a resulting injury. The first two statements of the Greaves holding and precedent are within the permissible spectrum of adversarial argument by lawyers and of judicial decision-making. The third statement is arguably within this spectrum. This fourth and final statement, however, is beyond the usual spectrum.

As this postscript demonstrates, there is considerable, but not unfettered, flexibility for argument and for decision-making in interpreting a holding and precedent. This postscript exemplifies additional functions of trial and appellate judges. A sophisticated understanding of using cases for legal reasoning requires an acquaintance with these functions, including the following.

Trial Judges' Discretion

Stare Decisis

1) Trial judges exercise a substantial and inescapable discretion in deciding whether or not the facts and issues presented in a new case

are similar to the facts and issues in a prior case cited as a precedent. There is no exact calculus or formula to apply in making this determination. Experience and lawyerly discretion are the guides. The application of the doctrine of stare decisis requires this exercise of discretion by the trial court. If the judge in exercising his discretion finds that the facts and issues are distinguishable (i.e., not similar), the precedent from the old case from the same or superior court is not controlling for the decision of the new case.

Extending and Limiting Precedent

2) If the trial judge in exercising his discretion finds, however, that the facts and issues in the old case from the same or superior court are similar to the new case, the doctrine of stare decisis requires that the precedent derived from the prior case be controlling. Nevertheless, the judge again exercises significant discretion in deciding exactly how to apply a judge-made rule contained in the holding of the prior case to the new case. In applying such a rule, a judge has the power to extend or limit the rule in applying it to the facts of the new case, and attorneys for both sides will be arguing for narrow versus broad, limiting versus extending interpretations. For example, the first, above-cited statement of the Greaves holding could then be extended in the ascending abstractions of the second and third statements of the Greaves holding. The judge in a new case could select one of the more general statements of the holdings even if the court in Greaves narrowly articulated the holding. The judge in a new case is not bound by a narrow statement of a prior holding or by a broad statement. In addition, in Greaves and in a good many other cases, the holding is not explicitly stated -- it is implicit. This fact also encourages varying articulations by opposing lawyers, as well as by judges, of the case holding, of what the case "really stands for." With this insight into the power of judges to extend or limit a precedent, you can avoid a beginner's befuddlement because statements of a judge-made rule often vary somewhat from case to case. That variation is the expectation in the common law system, not an idiosyncratic deviation.

Two or More Applicable Rules

3. In addition to the above-explained exercises of discretion, a trial judge also has the power to decide which of two or more clearly or arguably applicable precedents presented by opposing lawyers should be applied to a new case. Contrary to what some beginners believe, there are many such cases. Again, experience and lawyerly discretion are the guides to such judicial decision-making, not any exact calculus.

Statutory Rules

4. In applying statutory rules, trial judges also exercise substantial discretion. When the legislators enact statutory rules which include such abstract, broad-spectrum words as "reasonable," "equitable," "just," "appropriate," or "rules of reason," the legislature, in effect, invites judges to exercise a broad discretion in applying such rules so as to effect the policies intended by the legislators. When the legislators, in contrast, enact statutory rules which include more

concrete, narrow-spectrum words, such as "transporting" a "motor vehicle" in "interstate commerce," "knowing it" to have been "stolen," the legislators are prescribing more detailed direction to trial judges who apply such statutory rules. As McBoyle shows, however, even apparently clear words such as "motor vehicle" can pose an issue when applied to a particular fact situation. In addition, just as trial judges must exercise discretion in the cases where two or more clearly or arguably applicable judge-made rules are presented by opposing lawyers, so too the trial judge must exercise similar discretion where two or more such statutory rules are presented.

Words Are Ambiguous

5. Trial judges must also exercise substantial discretion because facts, rules, precedents, principles and policies are expressed in words, and words are intrinsically a storehouse of ambiguity. Beware the one-word-one-meaning fallacy. Determining which one of the multiple meanings of a word is intended requires analysis of the word as part of a rule, precedent, principle or policy in light of the specific facts and issues in a particular case. Sauer and Greaves illustrate the ambiguity in the broad-spectrum word "reasonable." McBoyle illustrates the ambiguity in the apparently clear, narrow-spectrum word "motor vehicle." This intrinsic ambiguity of words helps to make the law dynamic, not static, to make it fun and a challenge, not boring.

Appellate Judges' Discretion

In addition to trial judges' discretion, appellate judges also exercise substantial and inescapable discretion in deciding appeals based on claims that trial judges have abused their discretion in determining whether or not facts and issues are distinguishable, whether precedent should be extended or limited, whether one judge-made or statutory rule should have been selected over another, whether rules with broad or narrow language have been correctly applied, and whether the meaning of words have been correctly determined. If the appellate judges are in the highest state appellate court, not the intermediate appellate court, their decision is usually conclusive. Judges in inferior courts, trial courts and any intermediate appellate courts are bound by the decision of the highest court in the jurisdiction on the legality of exercise of trial court discreton.

Slot Machines and Digestion

First-year students often react with dismay at the discovery that trial and appellate judges exercise substantial and inescapable discretion in applying and interpreting legal rules from cases and statutes. The dismay arises because of the shattering of a false image of judges as slot-machine automatons into whom facts are fed and out of whom spew rules and decisions. To the contrary, lawyers, legislators, trial and appellate judges make and remake the law in a living, ever-unfolding process. The law respects the past, but is not its prisoner. The law respects logic and precedent, but is more than a closed logical system locked into adherence to rigid precedent.

The shattering of the slot-machine automaton image of judges often leads to another equally misleading image: that judges do whatever they want to do; that their discretion is unfettered; that decisions depend exclusively on their digestion, love life, politics and prejudices. While there is some truth here and some bizarre judges exist, including bigots, psychotics, neurotics and egomaniacs, this image is an exaggeration.

What it overlooks is that institutional restraints also exist. Decisions of trial and intermediate appellate judges may be appealed. Most decisions of the highest appellate courts may also be changed by legislative action. Moreover, most judges are influenced by their legal training and by their experience as lawyers and judges to decide within a spectrum of acceptable reasoning and decision-making. In addition, most judges have a regard for their professional reputation among other judges, lawyers and commentators, and don't want to be reversed. Accordingly, most judges conscientiously strive to exercise their judicial discretion within legal boundaries.

What the beginning law student doesn't know is that those boundaries allow considerable flexibility for resourceful lawyers to argue and resourceful judges to decide. Judicial decision-making is like being on a cruise ship in the Atlantic. You can choose to go swimming in the pool, play ping pong or snooze on the deck. The ship, itself, however, defines the boundaries of your choices, unless you decide to jump into the sea.

Discretion and Change

Do you see how this exercise of significant discretion by both trial and appellate judges allows gradual change in the law to accommodate the facts and claims urged by parties in new cases? The law incorporates respect for the river of cases from the past but it also allows judges a role in changing the law. The exercise of judicial discretion manifests the tension between the role of the law both in respecting the past and in accommodating the need to deal with new problems and evolving values. Understanding this creative tension in the law can help you to understand why rules and reasoning concerning the same issues may vary, especially over time. Rules and reasoning evolve as rules and reasoning are applied. Hence, this jurisprudential sounding point is quite practical: it sheds light on what is happening in the cases.

I. INTRODUCTION

In Sauer and Greaves in the last chapter, lawyers and judges engaged in a routine, every day disagreement about the application of an undisputed, but somewhat vague element (the standard of reasonable care) of a legal rule of tort negligence, to a set of facts whose legal significance is quite disputable. Were the key facts that the playing of "ring-a-levio" on the sloping, wet, grassy area next to the pool created an added, unreasonable risk? Or were the key facts that this game had inherent risks against which tort law should not, and cannot, protect? To call the disagreement over these facts a "routine, every day disagreement" is not to slight its importance. The conflict was of pressing weight for the plaintiffs and defendants, for their attorneys, and, judging by the tone of the opinions, for the judges too.

In Woods v. Lancet (303 N.Y. 349 [1951]), discussed in this chapter, you will not see any conflict over which facts are key. Instead, the dispute is centered on whether an entrenched, common law (judge-made) rule of tort negligence should be affirmed or overturned. While appellate courts do not decide such issues every day, this type of case is a legal landmark and is the type frequently printed in casebooks used in law schools. Understanding the types of justification embodied in Judge Desmond's skillfully crafted opinion for the New York State Court of Appeals provides insight into the variety of types of reasoning typically employed in such landmark cases and in some other cases. In briefing Woods, apply the six-step approach with the guidelines and try especially to identify, categorize and understand the significance of these types of reasoning.

II. ROBERT C. WOODS, an Infant, by ESTELLE WOODS, His Guardian Ad Litem, Appellant, v. JOSEPH LANCET, Respondent.

Argued October 4, 1951; decided December 6, 1951

Woods v. Lancet, 278 App. Div. 913, reversed.

APPEAL from a judgment of the Appellate Division of the Supreme Court in the first judicial department, entered July 3, 1951, affirming, by a divided court, an order of the Supreme Court at Special Term (HAMMER, J.) in favor of defendant, entered in Bronx County, granting a motion by defendant for a dismissal of the complaint for failure to state a cause of action.

* * *

DESMOND, J. The complaint served on behalf of this infant plaintiff alleges that, while the infant was in his mother's womb during the ninth month of her pregnancy, he sustained, through the negligence of defendant, such serious injuries that he came into this world permanently maimed and disabled. Defendant moved to dismiss the complaint as not stating a cause of action, thus taking the position that its allegation, though true, gave the infant no right to recover damages in the courts of New York. The Special Term granted the motion and dismissed the suit, citing Drobner v. Peters (232 N.Y. 220). In the Appellate Division one Justice voted for reversal with an opinion in which he described the obvious injustice of the rule, noted a decisional trend (in other states and Canada) toward giving relief in such cases, and suggested that since Drobner v. Peters (supra) was decided thirty years ago by a divided vote, our court might well re-examine it.

The four Appellate Division Justices who voted to affirm the dismissal below, wrote no opinion except that one of them stated that, were the question an open one and were he not bound by Drobner v. Peters (supra), he would hold that "when a pregnant woman is injured through negligence and the child subsequently born suffers deformity or other injury as a result, recovery therefor may be allowed to the child, provided the causal relation between the negligence and the damage to the child be established by competent medical evidence." (278 App. Div. 913.) It will hardly be disputed that justice (not emotionalism or sentimentality) dictates the enforcement of such a cause of action. The trend in decisions of other courts, and the writings of learned commentators in the period since Drobner v. Peters was handed down in 1921, is strongly toward making such a recovery possible. The precise question for us on this appeal is: shall we follow Drobner v. Peters, or shall we bring the common law of this State, on this question, into accord with justice? I think, as New York State's court of last resort, we should make the law conform to right.

Drobner v. Peters (supra), like the present case, dealt with the sufficiency of a complaint alleging prenatal injuries, tortiously inflicted on a nine-month foetus, viable at the time and actually born later. There is, therefore, no material distinction between that case and the one we are passing on now. However, Drobner v. Peters must be examined against a background of history and of the legal thought of its time and of the thirty years that have passed since it was handed down. Early British and American common law gives no definite answer to our question, so it is not profitable to go back farther than Dietrich v. Northampton (138 Mass. 14), decided in 1884, with an opinion by Justice HOLMES, and, apparently, the first American case. Actually that was a death case, since the five-month infant, prematurely born, survived for a few minutes after birth. The principal ground asserted by the Massachusetts Supreme Court (138 Mass., at p. 17) for a denial of recovery was that "the unborn child was a part of the mother at the time of the injury" and that "any damage to it which was not too remote to be recovered for at all was recoverable by her" (the mother). A few years later (1890), in Ireland, the Queen's Bench Division, in a very famous holding, refused to allow a suit to be brought on behalf of a child born deformed as the result of an accident in defendant's railway coach, two of the Justices taking the ground that the infant plaintiff was not in esse at the time of the wrong, and the other two regarding the suit as one on the contract of carriage with no duty of care owing by the carrier to the unborn infant whose presence was unknown to defendant (Walker v. Great Northern Ry. of Ireland, 28 L. R. Ir. 69). A similar complaint was dismissed for similar reasons, and the dismissal affirmed by the Appellate Division, Second Department, in Nugent v. Brooklyn Heights R. R. Co. (154 App. Div. 667, appeal dismissed 209 N. Y. 515). It is significant that the Appellate Division's opinion in the Nugent case (supra) indicates that, had it not been for the contract-of-carriage theory and its supposed consequences, the writer of the opinion would have favored recovery. Other strong support for just treatment of prenatal wrongs (of another kind) is found also in the 1893 opinion of Justice HAIGHT (later of this court) in Quinlen v. Welch (69 Hun 584); however, on appeal, this court found it unnecessary to pass on the point (141 N. Y. 158). There were, in the early years of this century, rejections of such suits by other courts, with various fact situations involving before-birth traumas (see Allaire v. St. Luke's Hosp., 184 Ill. 359); Gorman v. Budlong, 23 R. I. 169; Stanford v. St. Louis-San Francisco Ry. Co., 214 Ala. 611; Newman v. City of Detroit, 281 Mich. 60; Magnolia Coca Cola Bottling Co. v. Jordan, 124 Tex. 347; Buel v. United Rys. Co., 248 Mo. 126; Lipps v. Milwaukee Elec. Ry. & Light Co., 164 Wis. 272) and, quite recently, Massachusetts has reaffirmed the Dietrich rule (Bliss v.Passanesi, 326 Mass. 461). The movement toward a more just treatment of such claims seems to have commenced with the able dissent in the Allaire case (supra), which urged that a child viable but in utero, if injured by tort, should, when born, be allowed to sue; and the movement took impetus from the Wisconsin court's statement in the Lipps opinion (supra), that it was restricting its holding (of nonrecovery) to a nonviable child. Thus, when Drobner v. Peters came to this court in 1921, there had been no decisions upholding such suits, although the two New York lower court rulings above cited (Nugent and Quinlen cases, supra) were favorable to the position taken by plaintiff here.

In Drobner v. Peters (supra), this court, finding no precedent for maintaining the suit, adopted the general theory of Dietrich v. Northampton (supra), taking into account, besides the lack of authority to support the suit, the practical difficulties of proof in such cases, and the theoretical lack of separate human existence of an infant in utero. It is not unfair to say that the basic reason for Drobner v. Peters was absence of precedent. However, since 1921, numerous and impressive affirmative precedents have been developed. In California (Scott v. McPheeters, 33 Cal. App. 2d 629) the Court of Appeal allowed the suit -- reliance was there put on a California statue but that statute was not directly in point, since it directed only that "a child conceived, but not yet born, is to be deemed an existing person, so far as may be necessary for its interests in the event of its subsequent birth." That California statute merely codified an accepted and ancient common-law rule (see Stedfast v. Nicoll, 3 Johns, Cas. 18, 23, 24) which, for some reason, has not, at least in our court, been applied to prepartum injuries tortiously inflicted. In 1949, the Ohio Supreme Court (Williams v. Marion R. T., Inc., 152 Ohio St. 114, rule affirmed by the same court in Jasinsky v. Potts, 153 Ohio St. 529) and Minnesota's highest tribunal (Verkennes v. Cornica, 229 Minn. 365), and in 1951, the Court of Appeals of Maryland (Damasiewicz v. Gorsuch, ___ Md. ___ 79 A.2d 550) and the Supreme Court of Georgia (Tucker v. Carmichael, 208 Ga. 201) upheld the right of an infant to bring an action like the one we are here examining, without statutory authorization. The Supreme Court of Canada had announced the same rule back in 1933 (Montreal Tramways v. Leveille, [1933] 4 Dom.L.Rep. 337). In New Jersey a strong five-to-ten dissent (written by the Chief Justice) unsuccessfully urged the same view (Stemmer v. Kline, 128 N. J. L. 455 [1942]). In England there seems to be no controlling precedent (see Professor Winfeld's comprehensive article in 4 U. of Toronto L. J. [1941-42] 285 et seq.). Of law review articles on the precise question there is an ample supply (see 20 Minn. L. Rev. [Feb., 1936] 321-322; 34 Minn. L. Rev. [Dec., 1949] 65-66; 48 Mich. L. Rev. [Feb., 1950] 539-541; 35 Cornell L. Q. [Spring, 1950] 648-654; 1951 Wis. L. Rev. [May] 518-528; 50 Mich. L. Rev. [Nov., 1951] 166-167). They justify the statement in Prosser on Torts, at page 190, that: "All writers who have discussed the problem have joined in condemning the existing rule, in maintaining that the unborn child in the path of an automobile is as much a person in the street as the mother, and urging that recovery should be allowed upon proper proof."

What, then, stands in the way of a reversal here? Surely, as an original proposition, we would, today, be hard put to it to find a sound reason for the old rule. Following Drobner v. Peters (supra) would call for an affirmance but the chief basis for that holding (lack of precedent) no longer exists. And it is not a very strong reason, anyhow, in a case like this. Of course, rules of law on which men rely in their business dealings should not be changed in the middle of the game, but what has that to do with bringing to justice a tort-feasor who surely has no moral or other right to rely on a decision of the

New York Court of Appeals? Negligence law is common law, and the common law has been molded and changed and brought up-to-date in many another case. One court said, long ago, that it had not only the right, but the duty to re-examine a question where justice demands it (Rumsey v. New York & N.E.R.R. Co., 133 N. Y. 79, 85, 86, and see Klein v. Maravelas, 219 N. Y. 383). That opinion notes that Chancellor KENT, more than a century ago, had stated that upwards of a thousand cases could then be pointed out in the English and American reports "'which had been overruled, doubted or limited in their application,'" and that the great Chancellor had declared that decisions which seem contrary to reason "'ought to be examined without fear, and revised without reluctance, rather than to have the character of our law impaired, and the beauty and harmony of the system destroyed by the perpetuity of error.'" And Justice SUTHERLAND, writing for the Supreme Court in Funk v. United States (290 U.S. 371, 382), said that while legislative bodies have the power to change old rules of law, nevertheless, when they fail to act, it is the duty of the court to bring the law into accordance with present day standards of wisdom and justice rather than "with some outworn and antiquated rule of the past." No reason appears why there should not be the same approach when traditional common-law rules of negligence result in injustice (See Hagopian v. Samuelson, 236 App. Div. 491, 492, and see Justice STONE'S article on "The Common Law in the United States," 50 Harv. L. Rev. [1936], pp. 4-7).

The sum of the argument against plaintiff here is that there is no New York decision in which such a claim has been enforced. Winfeld's answer to that (see U. of Toronto L. J. article, supra, p. 29) will serve: "if that were a valid objection, the common-law would now be what it was in the Plantagenet period." And we can borrow from our British friends another mot: "When these ghosts of the past stand in the path of justice clanking their medieval chains the proper course for the judge is to pass through them undeterred" (Lord ATKIN in United Australia, Ltd., v. Barclay's Bank, Ltd., [1941] A. C. 1, 29). We act in the finest common-law tradition when we adapt and alter decisional law to produce common-sense justice.

The same answer goes to the argument that the change we here propose should come from the Legislature, not the courts. Legislative action there could, of course, be, but we abdicate our own function, in a field peculiarly nonstatutory, when we refuse to reconsider an old and unsatisfactory court-made rule. Perhaps, some kinds of changes in the common law could not safely be made without the kind of factual investigation which the Legislature, and not the courts, is equipped for. Other proposed changes require elaborate research and consideration of a variety of possible remedies -- such questions are peculiarly appropriate for Law Revision Commission scrutiny, and, in fact, the Law Revision Commission has made an elaborate examination of this very problem (1935 Report of N.Y. Law Revision Commission, pp. 449-476). That study was made at the instance of the late Chief Judge POUND of this court and was transmitted to the Legislature by the commission. Although made before the strong trend in favor of recovery had clearly manifested itself, the Law Revision Committee's comments were strongly in favor of the position taken in this opinion. The report, itself, contained no recommendations for legislation on the subject but that apparently was because the commission felt that it was for the courts to deal with this common-law question. At page 465, for instance, the report said: "The common law does not go on the theory that a case of first impression presents a problem of legislative as opposed to judicial power."

Two other reasons for dismissal (besides lack of precedent) are given in Drobner v. Peters (supra). The first of those, discussed in many of the other writings on the subject herein cited, has to do with the supposed difficulty of proving or disproving that certain injuries befell the unborn child, or that they produced the defects discovered at birth, or later. Such difficulties there are, of course, and, indeed, it seems to be commonly accepted that only a blow of tremendous force will ordinarily injure a foetus, so carefully does nature insulate it. But such difficulty of proof or finding is not special to this particular kind of lawsuit (and it is beside the point, anyhow, in determining sufficiency of a pleading). Every day in all our trial courts (and before administrative tribunals, particularly the Workmen's Compensation Board), such issues are disposed of, and it is an inadmissible concept that uncertainty of proof can ever destroy a legal right. The questions of causation, reasonable certainty, etc., which will arise in these cases are no different, in kind, from the ones which have arisen in thousands of other negligence cases decided in this State in the past.

The other objection to recovery here is the purely theoretical one that a foetus in utero has no existence of its own separate from that of its mother, that, is, that it is not "a being in esse." We need not deal here with so large a subject. It is to be remembered that we are passing on the sufficiency of a complaint which alleges that this injury occurred during the ninth month of the mother's pregnancy, in other words, to a viable foetus, later born. Therefore, we confine our holding in this case to prepartum injuries to such viable children. Of course such a child, still in the womb is, in one sense, a part of its mother, but no one seems to claim that the mother, in her own name and for herself, could get damages for the injuries to her infant. To hold, as matter of law, that no viable foetus has any separate existence which the law will recognize is for the law to deny a simple and easily demonstrable fact. This child, when injured, was in fact, alive and capable of being delivered and of remaining alive, separate from its mother. We agree with the dissenting Justice below that "To deny the infant relief in this case is not only a harsh result, but its effect is to do reverence to an outmoded, timeworn fiction not founded on fact and within common knowledge untrue and unjustified." (278 App. Div. 913, 914.)

The judgments should be reversed, and the motion denied, with costs in all courts.

Contrast your brief of Woods with the excellent brief set forth below.

III. AN EXCELLENT BEGINNER'S BRIEF

Facts

Infant-P's complaint alleged that while viable in mother's womb in 9th month of mother's pregnancy, D negligently inflicted "such serious injuries" that upon birth the P was "permanently maimed and disabled."

Comment: This statement of facts is as precise, succinct and conclusory as the court's statement of the facts. Note the severity of the claimed injuries.

P's c/a f/neg. tort against D barred by precedent from Drobner v. Peters (1921) in the same court: infant-P has no c/a f/neg. tort f/injuries neg. inflicted by D while infant was a viable foetus.

Comment: In Woods, an entire rule, rather than an element of a rule, or particular language, was at stake.

Procedural History

D's motion to dismiss P's complaint before trial as legally insufficient granted by trial court on ground that facts alleged in said complaint, even if all regarded as true, did not establish a recognized c/a. P had no rt. to a c/a, based on authority of Drobner v. Peters. App. Div. affirmed, one judge dissenting. Case now in N.Y.S. Ct. of Appeals (highest appellate ct.).

Comment: While a clear understanding of the procedural situation is basic in briefing each case, here it was even more important in determining exact issue at stake: whether or not such infant-plaintiff should have a right to a cause-of-action and be authorized to prove his case at trial.

Issue

Should the precedent established by Drobner v. Peters which denied a cause-of-action in tort for the D's negligent infliction of injuries when the infant-P was a viable foetus in its mother's womb, be overruled as inconsistent with justice?

Comment: For your purposes, you should specify more precisely than Judge Desmond's short-hand articulation of the issue (see p. 112). It was all right for the judge, but it is too broad for you.

	Holding
An excellent formulation of the issue leads to an excellent formulation of the holding, which announced a new, common-law rule for this state.	It should be overruled: an infant has a cause-of-action in tort for the D's negligent infliction of injuries when the infant was a viable foetus in its mother's womb.
	Judgment
P won the right to a cause-of-action in negligent tort and had to prove his case at trial.	Judgment of the Appellate Division reversed (motion to dismiss P's complaint should be denied). (Case proceeds to trial, settlement, etc.).
	Reasoning
Unlike Sauer and Greaves in Chapter IV, the facts here in Woods were found by ct. to be "similar" to Drobner. Drobner was "on point".	First, the ct. concluded there was "no material distinction" between facts of Drobner v. Peters and Woods.
Student explicity articulates what court's opinion implied.	(Hence it wasn't possible to distinguish the two cases factually and thereby avoid application of precedent derived from Drobner holding. Applying stare decisis, this precedent ordinarily should have applied.)
The court's survey of legal thought leading to the holding in Drobner was not unimportant. It's clear objective was to lay a foundation for later rejection of the Drobner precedent.	Second, ct. surveyed the legal thought underlying the Drobner precedent. Key Mass. case in 1884 denied c/a: Dietrich v. Northampton. In Drobner in 1921, Ct. of Appeals adopted rule from Dietrich.
Of various reasons specified in Drobner for its holding, the court stressed lack of precedent as most important. Note that this lack of precedent referred also to out-of-state cases and even to out-of-country cases. Such cases are persuasive, nonbinding authority on the New York Court of Appeals	Drobner ct.'s reasoning: no precedent (most important reason).

from the standpoint of stare decisis.

Note the court's logic: if lack of authority was the chief reason for the Drobner holding, that reason no longer existed. Why? "Numerous and impressive affirmative precedents" now existed. The Drobner precedent is analytically undermined by the removal of its main rationale.

The commentators (law writers), especially the influential Prosser, are marshalled for additional support.

This conclusion is manifestly a culminating step in the court's argument so far.

Ct. says in effect: stare decisis is fundamental but so is right & duty of highest state appellate court to change common law rule to accord with justice. Remember the interest at stake here: this infant "came into the world permanently maimed and disabled" by the defendant's negligence. This interest, (and other such future interests), provided a catalyst for the court's reasoning.

In our governmental system of separation of powers, the legislature and the court both have the power to alter such a judge-made rule. Court need not await legislative action. Legislative advantage in holding hearings, in listening to experts testify, and in doing research, is not pertinent here. Why?

1) Change is a matter of moral principle here: a claim of justice, not of utility or of fact.

Third, ct. contrasted lack of precedent prior to Drobner with "numerous & impressive affirmative precedents" after 1921 in many states and Canada.

Also many law review articles all agreed, e.g., Prosser: "all; writers" condemned old rule & urged creation of a c/a here.

Thus, "chief basis" for Drobner holding ("lack of precedent") no longer existed.

Fourth, ct. argued c.l. is dynamic, not static: ct. has rt. and duty to mold, change & modernize c.l. rules to serve "justice."

Fifth, ct. need not defer to remedial legis. action on "old" "unsatisfactory ct-made rule." Legis. & ct. both have power to change it. Moreover, N.Y.S Law Rev. Comm. has studied issue & recommended new rule.

2) In any event, the Law Revision Commission has already investigated and recommended changes.

Sixth, two other grounds for Drobner holding are rejected:

Alleged difficulties of proof present only routine difficulties handled every day.

A) No merit in argument of difficulties of proof, which are not greater here than in other tort cases, espec. Workmen's Comp. cases.

Courts decide only what they must decide. Courts are loath to decide broad theoretical issues presenting sweeping political, philosophical or theological beliefs. Courts usually decide cases on narrowest ground presented by facts and issue of particular controversy.

B) Ct. states that it is unnessary to deal with "purely theoretical" issue that foetus is not "'being in esse.'" Facts, issue and holding in this case refer only to legal sufficiency of complaint alleging a c/a for neg. injury to a viable foetus later born alive.

Note here that the holding is expressly confined to a viable foetus later born alive. Note too, however, that viability would arguably cover a foetus less than nine months (e.g., a seven-or-eight-month old foetus).

Comment

With experience and confidence, however, your statement of the reasoning might resemble the following.

Reasoning

1) Drobner v. Peters, 1921 Ct. App. case which denies c/a here is "on point" but ct. declines to follow it.

2) Drobner holding based mostly on "lack of precedent."

3) Since Drobner in 1921, num. and impress. precedent in

states & Canada, & support from commentators.

4) Hence, "lack of precedent" basis f/Drobner changed.

5) Ct. has power & duty to change old c.l. rule to serve "justice."

6) No merit to other Drobner arguments of diff. of proof (like other T cases); and to theoret. issue re foetus a "being in esse" (not necess. to decide).

IV. FUNCTIONS OF THE COURT EXEMPLIFIED IN WOODS

Stare Decisis and Justice

1. In Woods, you see a dramatic example of the highest court in a state, the New York State Court of Appeals, overruling an entrenched, thirty-year-old rule of its own making and establishing a contrary rule for all New York State courts. The drama rises in what the Court of Appeals does not explicitly address: subordinating the ordinary, day-to-day meaning of the doctrine of stare decisis. The court itself states that the facts in Woods present "no material distinction" from the facts in Drobner. It is elementary then that the rule incorporated in the Drobner holding ordinarily should apply. The drama emerges, too, from the fundamental policy interests entangled with stare decisis which might on the face of it seem to be sacrificed, including the following:

- -- our courts decide controversies according to a general rule, not on an ad hoc basis
- -- citizens may rely on established legal rules in ordering their business relations and in conducting their lives without fear that such rules will be "changed in the middle of the game"
- -- lawyers should be able to counsel those who seek their advice with reasonable certainty about established rules and with ability reasonably to predict which behavior will result in liability and which will not.

In this skillfully crafted opinion, the court does not systematically discuss these matters. It does not, however, neglect them altogether. Against the argument of reliance on rules for ordering commerce (and social life), Judge Desmond's court response is "...what has that to do with bringing to justice a tort-feasor who has no moral...right to rely on a decision of the" court? The judge here is referrig to the fact that the defendant appears to be a clear tortfeasor as to the mother's injuries. Implicit in this response is also a rejection of the possible argument that the court's decision slights the lawyer's role in counseling clients about established rules and in predicting which behavior will and will not result in liability. How could a tortfeasor such as the defendant here be so counseled or his liability predicted? Undoubtedly, Judge Desmond would also reject the first argument as inappropriate: no <u>ad hoc</u> decision-making was implied in the <u>Woods</u> holding or reasoning. <u>Woods</u> is decided by a holding that will apply to like cases in the future.

Judge Desmonds's opinion for the court persuasively illustrates that the fundamental doctrine of <u>stare decisis</u> does not mean that precedents must be slavishly followed. There are exceptions. As the opinion illustrates, there is excellent authority, indeed many precedents, for overruling old precedents "to bring the law into accordance with present day standards of wisdom and justice" (e.g., <u>Funk v. U.S.</u> 290 U.S. 371, 382). Following old precedents in new cases is not absolute. Hence, with a more sophisticated understanding of <u>stare decisis</u>, the argued conflict between the doctrine of <u>stare decisis</u> and the <u>Woods</u> holding fades away.

Inherent in the court's claim of the justice to be served in <u>Woods</u> is the principle that evolving conceptions of justice should be served by an evolving common law. The court here subordinated the following of precedent to a claim of justice. It would be foolhardy, however, to assume that precedent will always defer to justice. Precedent will triumph in at least some cases against a claim of justice. In addition, claims of utility -- of economic, social or political benefit for a majority or for a large number of people -- will also occasionally triumph against old precedents. Our law serves many fundamental interests (or objectives) which courts must balance or rank in order of preference and subordination. Again, there is no simple formula or calculus for such balancing or rank ordering.

<u>Distinguishing Two Different Kinds of Appeals</u>

2. In prior chapters, the appellate courts reviewed judgments of trial courts rendered after a trial. In <u>Woods</u>, the Court of Appeals reviewed a judgment of the intermediate appellate court which affirmed the judgment of the trial judge rendered without any trial. This trial court judgment was based on the pleadings of the parties, the complaint of the plaintiff and the answer of the defendant. The trial judge, because of the <u>Drobner</u> precedent, granted the defendant's motion to dismiss the plaintiff's complaint because it did not allege a theretofore

recognized cause-of-action for tort negligence. When the Court of Appeals overruled its Drobner precendent, it determined that the plaintiff's complaint did allege a recognized cause-of-action. This determination does not mean that a plaintiff automatically prevails. Not at all. The plaintiff must then proceed to try its case on the merits in the trial court. The plaintiff must establish the facts which spell out the elements of tort negligence. It is important for you to recognize the difference between an appeal based on claims of error after a trial of all the factual and legal issues, and an appeal, as in Woods, arising from a pre-trial granting of a motion to dismiss because of legal insufficiency of the plaintiff's pleadings, i.e., no recognized cause of action is alleged. In the latter situation, the plaintiff, if successful in the appellate court, must stll prove his factual and legal allegations by a preponderance of the evidence in the trial court.

Woods thus illustrates also the significance in briefing of the procedural step: determining exactly what happened below and exactly who is appealing what claim of error. Figuring out the procedural status of the case helps you to unravel the meaning of the case -- to look backward to see its origin and, hence, to understand the current issue, holding, judgment and reasoning.

Interacting of Substantive and Procedural Law

3. Woods also illustrates the interaction of substantive and procedural law. Substantive rules are ordinarily applied because of procedural triggers. For example, the trial court initially applied, as it must, the substantive rule embodied in the clear Drobner precedent and granted the defendant's procedural motion to dismiss the plaintiff's complaint because it did not state a then recognized cause-of-action. After the Court of Appeals overruled its old Drobner precedent, however, the trial court then applied, as it must, the new substantive rule embodied in the Court of Appeals' holding. Any subsequent procedural motion by the defendant to dismiss the plaintiff's cause-of-action would, of course, be denied because of the new precedent established by the Court of Appeals. The broadly applicable conclusion is that substantive rules are often applied in trial courts in response to procedural motions - e.g., a motion to dismiss the complaint, or a motion for a directed verdict (as in Port Huron, p. 78).

The Court In Woods Need Not Defer to the Legislature

4. Judge Desmond emphasized in the Woods opinion that both the state legislature and the Court of Appeals have the power to overturn the Drobner precedent. Since the Drobner precedent is judge-made, the Court of Appeals, as the highest appellate court in New York, need not defer here to the state legislature. Suppose for a moment, however, that the rule imposed by Drobner was imposed, instead, by a state statute. The Court of Appeals would then have no power to overturn the statutory rule. Why? Only the legislature which enacted the statute has the power to overturn it. With a statutory rule, the judicial power is to interpret and apply the rule, not to overturn it. In rare cases, the judicial power extends to invalidating a statute which is in conflict with a constitutional provision ("the fundamental law"). Contrary

to what some beginning students believe, most courts rarely do so and for a most compelling reason: in a democratic system of government, a legislature's expression of the popular will should not lightly be disregarded.

Stare Decisis and Res Judicata

5. Even though the New York Court of Appeals in Woods in 1951 overruled its prior holding in Drobner v. Peters, the Court of Appeals did not reverse the judgment of Drobner rendered in 1921. That judgment survived the change of the rule and remained undisturbed. The reason is that the doctrine of res judicata applies (see p. 6) and bars retroactive invalidation of the judgment, even though the rule embodied in the Drobner holding was rejected by the Court of Appeals in Woods. What is illustrated is that the doctrine of res judicata is applied quite strictly by the courts. Without this strict application, the policy served by the doctrine -- promoting authoritative and final decision of controversies -- would be undermined. In contrast, as Woods illustrates, the doctrines of stare decisis is more flexibly applied. In addition, in constitutional law cases, the application of the doctrine of res judicata is more complicated.

V. ISSUES NOT CONSIDERED AND DECIDED IN WOODS

Issues	Answers
A) Whether this claim of justice was well grounded in social theory and moral philosophy?	Not necessary for the court's decision. Its power to entrench a claim of justice into judge-made law does not require that the claim be well recognized in social theory and moral philosophy. Law, social theory and philosophy are not identical.
B) Whether this conclusory claim of justice should have been detailed?	Not necessary to do so for simple reason that no judge on the court cared to dispute it.
C) Whether the foetus here was a human being for all legal purposes?	Irrelevant -- even a model illustration of what legal reasoning is not: a sweeping issue leading to a sweeping standard.
D) Whether abortion is justified?	Irrelevant to the decision of this case.
E) Whether the creation of the cause-of-action for the infant here was warranted on a cost-benefit analysis?	Irrelevant. The right to a cause-of-action here was grounded on a claim of justice. Cost benefit analysis was not raised.

F) Whether public opinion and the legislature approved of this decision and reasoning?

Irrelevant. Judicial decision-making does not require majority, or even minority, support.

G) Whether this family was affluent and therefore did not need money damages?

Irrelevant. The cause-of-action is the plaintiff's, not the family's. In addition, there is no means test for the assertion of legal rights. A billionaire and an indigent both have the same formal right to a cause-of-action.

H) Whether the mother here could have avoided this injury by taking another mode of transportation?

Irrelevant. An accurate crystal ball is not a prerequisite to the assertion of a legal claim.

I) Whether the defendant breached his legal duty owed to the plaintiff?

Wrong. The Court of Appeals decided that the defendant owed the infant plaintiff a legal duty. The trial court must decide whether or not the defendant breached this duty, an element in establishing tort negligence.

J) Whether the defendant's behavior caused (meaning both factual and legal cause) the plaintiff's injuries?

Wrong. The trial court must decide this element of the plaintiff's cause-of-action for tort negligence.

K) Whether the plaintiff was truly "permanently maimed and disabled" from the injury?

Wrong. The trial court must decide this matter.

L) Whether the display of the "permanently maimed and disabled" infant will influence the trial jury and prejudice the defendant?

I hope it did. It is only unfair prejudice that may result in legal error. It is perfectly proper to prove the injuries by showing the baby at trial.

If you can understand why these issues were not considered by the New York Court of Appeals in deciding Woods, you are gaining an awareness of the kinds of issues which are considered on appeal and the kinds of issues which are resolved in the trial court. Cultivating this awareness is essential for deciphering appellate cases and deepening your capacity to do legal reasoning.

VI. A FEW FINAL DEFINITIONS

1. Decisional law. This is a synonym for case law (see pp. 4-5).

2. Cause-of-action. A cause-of-action is a legal claim recognized by the law of a jurisdiction (state or federal), alleging a harm resulting from a violation of a legal duty for which the law provides a remedy (e.g., money damages, specific enforcement of a contract, or an injunction commanding action or forbearance). In Woods, the cause-of-action was for negligent tort and the remedy sought was money damages.

3. Sufficiency of the Complaint. In challenging the legal sufficiency of the complaint, a defendant claims that the complaint does not allege a cause-of-action, i.e., that the allegations of fact and law in the complaint do not constitute a recognized legal claim in a particular state or on the federal level. In a challenge to the legal sufficiency of a complaint, all the allegations of fact in the complaint are regarded as true. In deciding such a matter, a judge does no fact-finding. In Woods, the defendant moved to dismiss the plaintiff's complaint as insufficient on the basis that New York case law at that time provided "the infant no right to recover damages in the Courts of New York" -- that, even conceding arguendo, that the plaintiff's assertion of facts was proved, no cause-of-action would exist because of the precedent established by Drobner.

VII. VALUE OF PRECEDENTS

In addition to the overturning of a precedent by the highest appellate court in a jurisdiction, illustrated in Woods, courts and lawyers utilize a variety of arguments either to give added weight to a precedent or to detract from its significance.

First, certain courts, from time to time, enjoy special expertise and respect in specific areas and their opinions, therefore, may be viewed as carrying added significance. The opinions of the Second Circuit of the United States Court of Appeals concerning securities have received special attention. Many such cases emerge from the Wall street financial community which is within the jurisdiction of the Second Circuit. The opinions of the United States Court of Appeals for the District of Columbia possessed added weight in the past in the area of administrative law. Some judges give added significance to opinions of state appellate courts which have enjoyed special prestige, including, for example, the New York Court of Appeals and the Supreme Court of California.

Second, sometimes you see references in cases to opinions by Holmes, Cardozo, Brandeis or Learned Hand. Some judges give opinions by such prestigious judges special attention. Third, some opinions refer to a "unanimous" decision by a particular appellate court. Unanimous decisions carry at least a bit more weight. Fourth, sometimes cases refer to a "frequently-cited" or "favorably-cited" or "frequently-followed" precedent. The implication is that the precedent is judicially popular and respected and should be applied by the court to which the argument is addressed. Lastly, some court opinions buttress their application of a precedent by also arguing that the precedent accords with sound principle or policy or both.

Have you noticed that none of these arguments addresses the legal validity of the precedent. Indeed, validity is presumed and the arguments address only weight and respect. Such arguments are designed to persuade a trial or appellate court to apply a precedent in a specific case. Such arguments may be decisive in cases where two or more precedents are clearly or arguably applicable (see p. 7). As precedents multiply, there is a rise in the number of new cases to which two or more precedents are clearly or arguably applicable. Hence, the increasing importance of these various arguments aimed at weight and respect is clear.

A variety of arguments are urged to detract from the weight or respect accorded a precedent. First, if the prior case articulated the holding implicitly, it may be difficult to extract the clear holding. Opposing lawyers will probably argue for different formulations (see p. 32). Second, if an appellate court agrees on the result, the judgment, but not on the holding and reasoning, precedent may be hard to determine. There may be several concurring opinions in which judges explain their views of the holdings and applicable reasoning and no single opinion may command majority support.

Third, a decision from an appellate court may be accorded less weight or respect if there was a dissent. Case references to a "sharply-divided court" or "a bare majority" manifest this weighting. The degree of negative weighting may depend on the reputation of the author of the dissent and its persuasive power. Some cases are distinguished by the illustrious quality of the dissent. Fourth, some appellate opinions are categorized as "per curiam" opinions, i.e., opinions of the court without an acknowledged author. Such opinions are often summary, specifying a judgment but omitting the facts, issue, holding and reasoning. Hence, the precedential value of "per curiam" opinions is usually slight.

Fifth, lawyers commonly seek to restrict a precedent by limiting it to its facts. The argument is that the facts are so extraordinary or bizarre that the precedent should be limited to the extraordinary or bizarre facts of the case. Thus, the facts in the current case are always distinguishable. Opposing counsel is unlikely to agree with this factual characterization. Sixth, appellate courts often multiply exceptions to a precedent before eventually overturning the precedent. The precedent endures despite the numerous exceptions, but its precedential weight is weakened.

These arguments are designed to persuade a court not to apply a particular precedent. Again, such arguments may be decisive if two or more clearly or arguably applicable rules are urged upon a court.

VIII. OPINIONS CAN BE FUN

If you believe judges to be devoid of wit, consider Justice Jackson's comments in McGrath v. Kristensen, 340 U.S. 162, 178 (1950), in which Jackson illustrates notable examples of reasons given by judges who declined to follow their own prior opinions.

> Baron Bramwell extricated himself...by saying 'The matter does not appear to me now as it appears to have appeared to me then.' Andrews v. Styrap, 26 L.T.R. (N.S.) 704, 706. And Mr. Justice Story, accounting for his contradiction of his own former opinion, quite properly put the matter: 'My own error, however, can furnish no ground for its being adopted by this Court....' United States v. Gooding, 12 Wheat. 460, 478. Perhaps Dr. Johnson really went to the heart of the matter when he explained a blunder in his dictionary -- 'Ignorance, sir, ignorance.' But an escape less self-depreciating was taken by Lord Westbury, who, it is said, rebuffed a barrister's reliance upon an earlier opinion of his Lordship: 'I can only say that I am amazed that a man of my intelligence should have been guilty of giving such an opinion.'

IX. A FEW FINAL SUGGESTIONS

Q. Well, I've finished your chapters. Am I an expert now in briefing and understanding cases?

A. No. Not at all. You are a beginner, not an expert.

Q. What must I do to become more expert?

A. To be an advanced beginner, you must brief hundreds of cases, participate in class discussion, and gradually hone your skills in legal reasoning.

Q. Is there more to legal reasoning than what you have presented here?

A. Lots more. This book presents an introduction to legal reasoning.

Q. What else should I read to learn more about legal reasoning?

A. It isn't reading that will light the path. It's performing. Nevertheless, with misgivings born of experience, I suggest the following readings. The danger in reading such excellent materials before you begin law school or in the first few weeks of it is that you'll compound the natural beginner's confusion. Be careful. I recommend, therefore, that you look at some of the following materials after six or eight weeks of law school.

<u>The Bramble Bush</u> by Karl Llewellyn

<u>The Nature of the Judicial Process</u> by Judge Benjamin Cardozo

<u>Case Analysis and Fundamentals of Legal Writing</u> by William Statsky and John Wernet

Q. Do you have any other recommendations?

A. Yes. Brief your assigned cases in the special notebooks with wide margins ("law ruled"). These notebooks are available in law bookstores. You brief on the right. In the substantial left margin, you take notes in class as your professor discusses the case. What is your professor's analysis of the case? Why has she or he assigned the case? While many opinions discuss a number of issues, your professor may have assigned the case only to present one issue. This one issue may relate to substantive law or to an illustration of a lawyerly skill. The analysis of the case in class will reveal professorial priorities. Go with the current of your professor's pedagogic strategy. Don't swim against that current.

Save space in the notebook at the end of your brief. When you complete your brief before class, ask -- what has this case added in light of the other cases you have studied in a specific segment of your professor's course? Don't assume that "added" refers only to knowledge of rules, principles and policies. Instead, give equal weight as you reflect on the case to such knowledge and to demonstration of skills in legal analysis revealed by the case. Check and revise your brief after the class discussion of the case. Again, let your professor be your guide. Keep in mind that each case is best seen as a link in a chain of cases (see p. 17). Understand the link in light of the chain.

While most "shortcuts" turn out to be "longcuts," I also suggest that after a month or two of law school you should experiment with briefing at least some of your cases in the casebook. Yes, right in the casebook. You own it. You can write on the pages.

How do you do this? Take the more straightforward cases, ones in which the facts are intelligible; the procedural history is clear; the issue and holding are explicitly stated, are accurate and not cryptic; the reasoning is at least fairly well organized. Brief these cases by bracketing the relevant facts and underlining only the key facts. Write an <u>F</u> in the margin next to the cluster(s) of underlined key facts. Place a <u>P</u> next to the statement of the procedural history. Underline the explicitly stated issue and holding and place an <u>I</u> and <u>H</u> in the margin next to this underlining. Put a <u>J</u> next to the statement of the court's judgment, generally at the end of the opinion. With the reasoning, you number the arguments one by one, underline their most important parts and place an R in the margin. You should also strive to characterize each type of argument (e.g., policy...; or legal principle...).

This briefing in the book works less well if the issue and holding are implicit and you must extract them and if the reasoning is confusingly presented and the facts are lengthy and rambling.

Experiment. Can you brief at least some of your cases in the casebook? Do you learn as much as when you write out your brief in your notebook? Can you still respond well in class? Do you save substantial time? Generations of law students have briefed at least some of their cases in the casebook. You can too.

What do you do with the time you save? Review. Synthesize. Outline. Sharpen your skills in study groups. Practice answering the problems set forth in the old exams of your professors. I detail these and other methods in How To Do Your Best On Law School Exams.

A parting word which may encourage you through the thicket of the first year. While it is true that many core lawyerly skills are not taught by the case method of instruction in law school (see p. 19), it is nonsense that law school is unrelated to the real world of lawyering. The typical priority in the first year is legal reasoning which is a real-world priority. Whatever form your lawyering might assume -- private practice, legal services, governmental work -- your skill in legal reasoning is a sine qua non. You will use it every day. This cardinal truth is in no way diminished by the observation that varied other skills are also necessary.

Adios.

APPENDIX A

Abbreviations for Briefing Cases

Below is an alpabetical list of abbreviations for use in briefing cases. Since your briefs are for your benefit, however, use whatever abbreviations help you. These abbreviations can give you ideas for other abbreviations.

A	agent
A.B.A.J.	American Bar Association Journal
adm'r	administrator
aff'd	affirmed
A.L.I.	American Law Institute
A.L.J.	Administrative Law Judge
A.L.R.	American Law Reports
answ.	answer
app., apps.	appendix(ices)
app. div.	appellate division
art., arts.	article(s)
assoc.	associate
atty.	attorney
att'y gen.	attorney general
B	buyer or beneficiary
bfp	bona fide purchaser
b/k	breach of contract
bk., bks.	book(s)
BNA	Bureau of National Affairs
brd	beyond a reasonable doubt
c/a	cause-of-action
CCH	Commerce Clearing House
cert.	certiorari
ch., chs.	chapter(s)
cir. ct.	circuit court of appeals (federal)
ct. app.	court of appeal(s) (state)
cir. ct. app.	circuit court of appeals (state)
city ct.	city court
civ. app.	civil appeals
civil pro.	civil procedure
C.J.	Corpus Juris
C.J.S.	Corpus Juris Segundum
c/l or c.l.	common law
C.M.A.	Court of Military Appeals
C.M.R.	Court of Military Review
compl.	complaint
comm.	committee
Cong.	Congress
cons.	constitutional
cr.	creditor
crim. app.	criminal appeals
crim. l.	criminal law
D	defendant
dam.	damages
deb.	debtor
def.	defense
dir. ver.	directed verdict
dist.	district
ev.	evidence
em.	employer
ee.	employee
edit.	edition
F.2d	Federal 2d
fam. ct.	Family Court
f/D	for defendant
f.m.	felony murder
f/P	for plaintiff
F.R.D.	Federal Rule Decisions
Ga. L. R.	Georgia Law Review
H	husband
H.R.	House Report
J.	judge, justice
J J.	judges, justices
judg.	judgment
juris.	jurisdiction
K	contract
L	landlord
liab.	liability
litig.	litigation
mag.	mag istrate
mot.	motion
Nat. L.J.	National Law Journal
neg.	negligence
N.L.R.B.	National Labor Relations Board

Appendix A Continued

no., nos.	numbers(s)	sur. ct.	surrogate's court
O	offer	Supp.	Supplement
Ord.	order	T	torts
P	plaintiff	t	trustee or tenant
p., pp.	pages(s)	uncon.	unconstitutional
p/f	prima facie	U.S.C.	United States Code
pld'g.	pleading	U.S.C.A.	United States Code Annotated
proc. l.	procedural law		
P.	Property (course)	U.S.D.Ct.	United States District Court
prop.	property		
pub.	public	U.S.L.W.	United States Law Week
reas. man	reasonable man	U.S.Sup.Ct.	United States Supreme Court
rev'd.	reversed		
S	seller	v.	versus
s/p	specific performance	ver.	verdict
sub. l.	substantive law	W	wife
sup. ct.	superior court	w/i	within
sup. jud. ct.	supreme judicial court	w/o	without

APPENDIX B

Other Books, Video Recordings and Audiotapes by Professor John Delaney

OTHER BOOKS

1) How To Do Your Best On Law School Exams; 1982, 156 pp., $12.95, available in most law bookstores.

This book, borne of many years of law school teaching, offers a systematic approach to studying for exams, doing outlines, avoiding blunders, and answering law exam problems. It includes actual exam problems with illustrative "A" and poor answers and comments explaining why answers are excellent or poor. This book is in a sixth printing.

2) Criminal Law: A Problem Solving Approach, 1986, 430, pp. $17.95, available in most law bookstores.

With hundreds of short problems and "A" answers, this book systematically presents the substantive criminal law from basics to complexities. The book can be used to: 1) learn the criminal law; 2) test your knowledge of different substantive areas; and 3) practice writing lawyerly answers to problems. The book is designed as a complement to casebooks which, despite other virtues, confusingly present the substantive law.

VIDEO RECORDINGS

3) The Fundamentals of Taking Law School Exams - Part I, approx. 2 hours, 1/2 or 3/4 inch, color, $275.00

This video recording, intended for law libraries and student bar associations, presents an introduction to the taking of law exams, a specification of the five exam skills that you must display; the five grading criteria by which you'll be graded; a series of common exam blunders to be avoided; and a detailing of study recommendations which will help you to prepare for exams.

Part II, approx. 2 hours, 1/2 or 3/4 inch, color, $275.00.

Part II details the Delaney Method for spotting issues on law exams, a step-by-step approach. Part II also specifies a method for organizing and writing lawyerly answers. Lastly, Part II specifies suggestions for outlining your courses and completing checklists designed to aid you with your exams. Part I and II may be purchased together for $475.00.

AUDIOTAPES

4) The Fundamentals of Taking Law School Exams, approx. 4 hours, $24.95.

These audiotapes, intended for first year law students and students experiencing difficulty with exams, are the audio recording from the above-mentioned video recordings. They cover the topics specified above in 3).

NOTES